DATE DUE

DAVID HUME

HIS THEORY OF KNOWLEDGE
AND MORALITY

by

D. G. C. MACNABB, M.A.

FELLOW AND LECTURER IN PHILOSOPHY,
PEMBROKE COLLEGE, OXFORD

Second Edition

ARCHON BOOKS

HAMDEN, CONNECTICUT

FIRST PUBLISHED 1951

SECOND EDITION 1966

PRINTED IN GREAT BRITAIN

CONTENTS

PART ONE

HUME'S ACCOUNT OF THE UNDERSTANDING

PREFACE TO SECOND EDITION

SINCE this book was written philosophy has moved on apace. Books have been published on epistemology, the philosophy of mind and on Hume, which have led me to form a somewhat different picture of Hume. I have principally in mind Ryle's "Concept of Mind",[1] Wittgenstein's "Philosophical Investigations",[2] Passmore's "Hume's Intentions",[3] R. H. Popkin's "History of Scepticism from Erasmus to Descartes",[4] Flew's "Hume's Philosophy of Belief"[5] and E. C. Mossner's "Life of David Hume".[6]

I would now wish to summarise Hume's enterprise and the reasons for his failures in the following way.

Hume was impressed by four things: the discordant and crazy conclusions of dogmatic metaphysicians and theologians, the logical strength of the arguments of the Sceptics, the successes of Newtonian science, and the importance of finding a satisfactory theory of morals.

Scepticism was an ancient school of philosophy which professed to supply its disciple with a counter-argument for every argument he would ever meet. Thus armed he could kiss his hand to controversy and live quietly in accordance with natural instincts and local custom, thus achieving the "*ataraxia*" which all ancient philosophies pursued. Rediscovered at the Renaissance in the works of Sextus Empiricus, these arguments provided weapons for both sides in the religious controversies of the Reformation. Each side used them to discredit the reasoning of its opponents and make room for its own brand of faith. But handy as these arguments were for theologians, they were an embarrassment to science, which claims to be founded not on faith, but on reason.

Hume's problem was so to use scepticism as to undermine

---

[1] Hutchinson, 1949.
[2] Basil Blackwell, 1953
[3] Cambridge University Press, 1952
[4] Martinus Nijhoff, The Hague, 1960.
[5] Routledge & Kegan Paul, 1961.
[6] Nelson, 1954.

theology and metaphysics, but safeguard science and secular morality. His solution may be stated as follows.

Arguments are only valid against arguments. Sceptical arguments therefore may be valid against arguments proposed to justify our trust in our senses, memory and the lessons of experience, but they are not valid against that trust itself, which is based on natural instincts indispensable to our survival. Instinct prevails against argument; "Nature by an . . . uncontrollable necessity has determined us to judge as well as to breathe and feel". Experimental science is but a refinement and extension of such judgements. Moreover it can be applied to the study of human nature. So applied it shows us the nature of deductive reasoning, based on the impossibility of conceiving a contradiction, and its application to experience through mathematics. It shows us the instinctive basis in habit-formation of all empirical inferences concerning causes and effects. It shows us how human ingenuity has devised political and moral institutions which by their appeal to the natural principles of self-love and sympathy preserve society, without which men cannot survive. All these are natural, indispensable and irresistible principles. In contrast to them stand credulity, superstition, wishful thinking and prejudice. These are indeed common and in some conditions irresistible. But they are neither necessary nor desirable; we should be happier without them, and those whom we call men of sense reject their influence when they detect it. They are also in another sense "unnatural" in that they depend on artificial causes, the artifices of priests and propagandists. Finally, unlike experience, they do not provide a single growing coherent picture of the world, but a welter of incompatible alternatives, and no means of deciding between them.

Metaphysics, theology and scepticism have this in common, that they arise when reasoning, whether deductive or analogical, is applied beyond the sphere of common life, to which alone it is adapted. Scepticism is the only member of the trinity that is useful, for it can serve as a reminder of the limitations of our faculties.

Such in outline is Hume's attempt to limit faith in order to make room for science. The essence of it is "naturalism", that is the treatment of the understanding as a natural function of the human species, subject to natural laws and conditions, adapted to natural needs and subject to natural infirmities. It is diametrically opposed to views like that of Descartes, who regarded the understanding as the power of an absolutely free will to assent or dissent according to or against the divine law of reason.

I have two main criticisms. First, the programme is in part unnecessary. The sceptical arguments are not all unanswerable. Hume uses two kinds, which he does not clearly distinguish. Those of the first kind open up logical gaps—the gap between any object or event and any other, between sensations and objects, between relations of ideas and matters of fact, and between either of these last and judgements of value. These arguments are sound and constitute Hume's major contributions to philosophy, notwithstanding the spate of criticism which they have recently received. These arguments pose the problem, how, if at all, the gap is to be spanned.

Quite different are the sceptical arguments Hume deploys to prove inherent contradictions in our understanding, for instance the "direct and total opposition between our reason and our senses", the reduction of all probabilities to zero by successive considerations of our fallibility, and the riddle of the unity of consciousness. These are sophistries, and the problem they pose is to spot the fallacy.

My second criticism is that Hume's naturalism is not naturalistic enough. His analyses of the instinctive processes underlying our judgements of perception, probability and morality are stated in terms of "impressions" and "ideas". These are treated not as natural functions of a flesh-and-blood animal, but as independent occurrences, many of them "not susceptible of local conjunction", and private to the person who has them. They are the fragmented relics of the "ghost in the machine", the immaterial soul-substance which Hume himself derides. They are not genuine empirical entities, but the stock in trade of a theory—the "Philosophy of Ideas". This is the error attacked in Ryle's "Concept of Mind", and it vitiates what I say in Part I, Chapters VIII and IX, as well as what Hume says about sense-perception, induction and personal identity. If we accept the view that all knowledge is either indubitable datum or deduction from such, and impressions (or sense-data) as the only indubitable data, the sceptic has won the game at the first move, and our world can only end up as a construction of the imagination.

Had Hume been consistently naturalistic, in keeping with the tone of his chapters on "the Reason of Animals", he might have seen that what nature does, when, for example, we see something, is not to force us to fill the gaps in our sensations with vivid images, but to enable us to accommodate our behaviour to the object by using our eyes. For this is surely all that happens, as far as we can tell, when a dog sees a rabbit, and, as Hume says, the account that suffices for an animal suffices for the same thing in a human being.

There is an historical error in the first edition of my book in Part I, Chapter III, Section 3, page 46. The pictures were in fact insured, thanks to the robust commonsense of the Head of the College.

There is also I think a clear error of interpretation on pages 202 and 203. Professor Flew ("Hume's Philosophy of Belief", Chapter VIII) has convinced me that Hume in the "Enquiry concerning Human Understanding", Section VIII, set out a decisive argument for the incompatibility of Theism and Determinism, and that the suggestions I make in mitigation of this argument are explicitly or implicitly rejected by Hume in the "Dialogues concerning Religion".

References to page numbers of the Treatise are to the Everyman Edition. References by paragraphs to the Enquiries are to the numbered paragraphs in L. A. Selby-Bigge's (second) edition (Oxford University Press, 1902).

In addition to the authors mentioned in the text and in the Bibliography, I am deeply indebted to Professor H. J. Paton for reading the entire manuscript and making many valuable suggestions, and to my wife for her assistance in correcting the proof and compiling the index.

BIOGRAPHICAL NOTE

In view of the abundance of biographies of Hume, I shall give only a short account of his life and personality.

Hume was born at Edinburgh in 1711, of a poor but well-connected family of landed gentry, his father owning an estate called "Ninewells" near Berwick. He passed through the ordinary course of education at Edinburgh University and was destined by his family for the law. But, to use his own words, he "was seized very early with a passion for literature" and "found an insurmountable aversion to everything but the pursuits of philosophy and general learning". Books on law were secretly neglected in favour of Cicero and Virgil.

After an unsuccessful attempt to gratify his family by going into a business in Bristol in 1734, he went to France to study in a country retreat, adopting a plan of life to which thereafter consistently adhered, by which "he made a very rigid frugality supply his deficiency of fortune". In France he composed the "Treatise of Human Nature" (between the ages of 23 and 26).

He returned to London in 1737 and published the Treatise in 1738. According to Hume's autobiography it "fell dead-born from the press". Nevertheless, the sales were considerable, and though it was published in three separate successive volumes, the third volume (Book III, "Of Morals") was accepted for publication in 1740. It also elicited a long and foolishly abusive review in the "History of the Works of the Learned", which probably seriously upset Hume's self-esteem, always distinctly tender in literary matters. The Treatise was published anonymously.

From 1737 to 1745 Hume lived with his mother and brother at Ninewells, recovering from the blow, re-learning Greek, and writing and publishing a small volume of "Essays, Moral and Political".

In 1745 Hume made an unsuccessful bid for the vacant chair of "Ethics and pneumatic philosophy" at Edinburgh, and accepted a vexatious appointment as resident tutor to the young Marquis of Annandale. This appointment fortunately only lasted a year, and soon afterwards the Marquis was certified insane.

In 1746 Hume had his only taste of military adventures; he accompanied General St. Clair as secretary on an abortive expedition directed against the coast of Brittany, and later, in the same capacity, on a diplomatic mission to Turin and Vienna. On the latter expedition he wore the uniform of an officer, in which, according to the Earl of Charlemont, he cut a very peculiar figure. The same authority gives us an account of Hume's personal appearance, which, he adds, belied his real character to an unparalleled extent. "His face was broad and fat, his mouth wide, and without any other expression than that of imbecility. His eyes vacant and spiritless, and the corpulence of his whole person was far better fitted to communicate the idea of a turtle-eating Alderman, than of a refined philosopher. His speech, in English, was rendered ridiculous by the broadest Scotch accent, and his French was, if possible, still more laughable".[1]

The "Enquiry concerning Human Understanding" was published in 1748, and the "Enquiry concerning the principles of Morals" in 1751. The latter he regarded as "incomparably the best" of all his works. Though more respectfully reviewed, in deference to Hume's reputation as author of the Essays, these publications attracted little more attention than the Treatise. Hume was mortified but not discouraged.

In 1752 Hume was appointed librarian to the Faculty of Advocates in Edinburgh and set up house with his sister in Edinburgh. He now turned his attention to History, a study facilitated by his access to the library. He wrote History back-

---

[1]Memoirs of Charlemont, I. 15.

wards; first "The History of Great Britain" in two volumes
(James I to the Revolution), published 1756; then the "History
of England under the House of Tudor" (1759); finally the
"History of England from the Invasion of Julius Cæsar to the
Accession of Henry VII " (1761). After writing these works,
which brought him fame and considerable wealth, Hume
contented himself with revising and correcting his works.

During the same period in which he wrote the histories,
Hume also published his "Natural History of Religion" and
his "Political Discourses", the latter work bringing him during
his lifetime an even greater reputation as an economist than
that of his illustrious friend, contemporary and compatriot
Adam Smith.

Hume, sociable, hospitable, witty, famous, vain but not
envious of merit in others, was now a leading figure in the
literary world of the period, which has left us such great names
as Adam Smith, Dr. Johnson, Bishop Butler, Gibbon and
Rousseau.

In 1763 Hume accompanied the Earl of Hertford, our
ambassador, to Paris, and was later appointed secretary to the
Embassy. In 1765 he was left "chargé d'affaires" for some
months, during a change of ambassadors, and fulfilled his
duties efficiently. He was a great social success in Paris society
and enjoyed himself very much, though we are told his French
accent did not improve. In 1769 he returned to Edinburgh.

In the spring of 1775 Hume became affected with cancer
of the bowels, and soon realised that he was not to recover.
Unshaken in his assurance of total extinction, suffering no
great pain, he faced and met his end in the approved Epicurean
spirit; all who saw him in his last days testify to the continuance
of his courtesy, affability, wit and kindness. He also continued
sending corrections of his works to the printers to the very last.
He died on the 25th of August, 1776. His "Dialogues concerning Natural Religion" (probably written mostly before
1751) and his autobiography were published after his death in
accordance with his will.

It is worth quoting from Hume's autobiography his
summing up of his own character. "I am, or rather was . . .
a man of mild disposition, of command of temper, of an open,

social, and cheerful humour, capable of attachment, but little susceptible of enmity, and of great moderation in all my passions. Even my love of literary fame, my ruling passion, never soured my temper, notwithstanding my frequent disappointments. My company was not unacceptable to the young and careless, as well as to the studious and literary; and, as I took a particular pleasure in the company of modest women, I had no reason to be displeased with the reception I met with from them".[1]

The last statement in this quotation is well illustrated by an incident recorded by Alexander Carlyle.[2] Mrs. Adam, mother of the famous architects, at first refused to entertain Hume, because of his " atheism". But after he had been brought to dine with her under a false name she said that she liked "the large, jolly man who sat next me" best of all her sons' friends, and, on learning his identity, withdrew her objections, saying "He is the most innocent, agreeable, facetious man I ever met with".

---

[1]Hume never married.
[2]The autobiography of Dr. Alexander Carlyle, 1722-1805.

INTRODUCTION

A MAN who wants a philosophy by which to live, may be compared to a man who wants a house to inhabit or a ship in which to make a voyage; and like them he requires in his expert advisers two different capacities, the creative capacity to produce a satisfying design, and the critical capacity to ensure the adequacy of the scantlings and the soundness of the materials and fastenings.

Hume is emphatically a philosopher of the critical kind. And his advice is essentially wholesome. What he tells us to do is to examine our own nature, and the character and limitations of our reason. We shall then not be tempted to adopt any pretentious systems of philosophy, designs specifying materials which are not to be found in human nature, towers and pinnacles for which we cannot provide support, and a general lofty magnificence which is not in accordance with the requirements of our nature, but serves only to gratify an unjustifiable intellectual pride.

To drop the metaphor and quote Hume's own words, "Philosophical decisions", he tells us in the penultimate section of the "Enquiry concerning the Human Understanding", "are nothing but the reflections of common life, methodised and corrected . . . " ; we "will never be tempted to go beyond common life, so long as we consider the imperfection of those faculties which we employ, their narrow reach, and their inaccurate operations. While we cannot give a satisfactory reason why we believe, after a thousand experiments, that a stone will fall or fire burn; can we ever satisfy ourselves concerning any determination, which we may form, with regard to the origin of worlds, the situation of nature, from, and to eternity ?"

Let us consider more closely what Hume can have meant when he said that philosophical decisions are nothing but the reflections of common life methodised and corrected. How has it come about that the innocent and reasonable endeavour to methodise and correct the "reflections of common life" has led to the invention of the tremendous metaphysical systems and the apparently insoluble metaphysical conundrums which we read of in the works of famous thinkers? And what is Hume's advice as to what we should do and what we should avoid in prosecuting this laudable endeavour?

In common life we find ourselves under a constant and unavoidable necessity of making deliberate decisions which may roughly be classified in the following way:

(1) We have to decide what are the observable circumstances in which we are placed at any given time.

(2) We have to decide what are the probable but unobservable circumstances in which we are placed at that time

(3) We have to decide what actions of ours are possible in those circumstances.

(4) We have to decide what will be the probable consequences of the various actions which are possible for us.

(5) We have to decide, in the light of the answers we have given to these four questions, which action it is best to take.

Philosophy begins when we try to formulate and reflect on the principles we apply in making these decisions.

At first sight perhaps the task will not seem very formidable. For making decisions of the first kind we accept the evidence of our senses, together with certain precautions against illusions and hallucinations, and aided by the refinements of measurement and calculation. For making decisions of the second, third and fourth kinds we accept the principle of induction, that rules which have been found to hold good in observed cases will also hold good in similar but unobserved cases.

It is when we come to decisions of the fifth kind that we usually first begin to experience difficulties. For there seems to be a wide choice of principles on which a man may decide questions of good and evil and right and wrong; and the wider our acquaintance with life, the more clear it is that some people adopt one principle and some another, or at least appear to.

It has usually happened, as it did among the Ancient Greeks, that philosophical enquiries arose when sceptical and revolutionary thinkers challenged the accepted principles for making moral decisions. But they have also arisen as a result of the challenging of accepted methods of deciding questions of fact; for instance when the use of auguries, divinations, astrology, and prophecies was challenged by the advocates of scientific enquiry.

Such challenges forced men to reflect on the principles by which they decided the questions of common life; to try to formulate them clearly, and finally to justify them. As soon as philosophy begins to attempt a selection between rival principles and a justification of its selection, it begins to manifest one of its two major characteristics; it appears as a recommendation of a way of life, a practical philosophy.

The other major characteristic that philosophy manifests is that of providing a reasoned account of the nature of the universe and of man's place in it. This feature of philosophy also arises naturally, because any principle of decision seems to imply some very general fact or facts about the nature of things. The use of the testimony of the senses seems to imply the existence of objects independent of the mind, but accessible to it through the senses. Induction seems to imply natural laws which determine events to a regular and reliable pattern. Moral decisions seem to imply some purpose in the scheme of things, or some objective standards of fittingness and unfittingness, or some needs inherent in the nature of man, which mark out for him goals and ideals more imperative than the gratification of the impulse of the moment. The next step in philosophy is to endeavour to define these presuppositions, and to give reasons for supposing them to be true. Thus philosophy appears as speculative metaphysics, an attempt to prove propositions about the very general nature of things.

What help has Hume to offer us in the choice of a philosophy of life and the difficulties it involves? It is very natural to be philosophical. To continue to decide questions of fact and questions of good and evil on principles which we can neither formulate nor justify is neither admirable nor comfortable nor safe. As Plato says, the unexamined life is not worth living.

But if we go to the professional philosophers for help we find that all is not well with philosophy as a science, as Hume tells us in the Introduction to the "Treatise of Human Nature".

"It is easy" he says "for one of judgement and learning to perceive the weak foundation even of those systems, which have obtained the greatest credit. . . . Principles taken upon trust, consequences lamely deduced from them, want of coherence in the parts and of evidence in the whole, these are everywhere to be met with in the systems of the most eminent philosophers, and seem to have drawn disgrace upon philosophy itself". Nor do we need to possess much judgement and learning to be aware that something is wrong. "Even the rabble without doors may judge from the noise and clamour which they hear, that all goes not well within. . . . Disputes are multiplied as if everything was uncertain". The situation is not much different today.

What is the cause of this trouble? Philosophers, we have said, try to justify (or, in some cases, to discredit) by argument, propositions which must be presupposed in any ordinary enquiry. They proceed, that is, as if beside the methods of observation, induction and deduction which we ordinarily employ, they had *other* methods by which they can establish or disprove those truths which the ordinary methods only presuppose.

Now, nobody really believes philosophers to possess or be able to acquire faculties or methods of arriving at truth other than those we normally employ. Some persons may have strange powers, but it is not the authority of mystical experience, clairvoyance or metempsychotic reminiscence which we require when we ask for a philosophy of life. Further, even if philosophers did possess such powers, they would be none the better off for philosophical purposes; for these philosophical powers and faculties would in turn need analysis and justification and so on *ad infinitum*.

The Rationalists had met this difficulty by claiming to

discharge the whole task of speculative and practical philosophy by the use of pure deductive reasoning. It is philosophers of this kind in whom Hume is mainly interested. Their claim, according to him, is false. For he shows beyond all question, and by arguments whose validity is independent of any dubious psychological premiss on which his system may appear to be based, that pure deductive logic can never establish any proposition asserting a matter of fact and existence, or decide a moral question. There is only one means of deciding questions of fact, he maintains; that is by consulting experience. Moral questions are ultimately questions of feeling.

In so far then as it is facts we require of a philosopher, Hume says he can only offer us facts about Human Nature, established by the Experimental Method. This method will show us how we do in fact form our ideas and how the understanding in fact works in making its theoretical and practical decisions. It will be clear, Hume thinks, from these facts, what are the limits of Human Enquiry. It will be clear that questions about "origins of worlds", and the ultimate causes of our sensations are beyond our capacity, for we have no experience to guide us, and only experience can decide questions of fact.

Having realised this, "when we see that we have arrived at the utmost extent of human reason, we sit down contented"; for, according to Hume, our desire for metaphysical knowledge will cease when we see that it is not to be had. "Despair has almost the same effect upon us with enjoyment" and "we are no sooner acquainted with the impossibility of satisfying any desire, than the desire itself vanishes". (Treatise, Introduction, p. 7.)

We may doubt whether even the majority of men have such a happy facility for reconciling themselves to disappointment as Hume here describes, presumably as the result of observation of his own very philosophic self. But still we must admit that, when a child cries for the moon, there is little we can do but explain that the moon is out of his reach—and provide him with more accessible sources of entertainment.

But before going on to ask what other more accessible satisfactions Hume would offer us, we must consider some difficulties about the Experimental Method and ask whether

B

it is really the only device on which Hume relies in answering our demands for philosophical reassurance.

The main objection that may be raised is that his use of the method is circular. By experimental observation and inductive generalisation he seeks to show that experimental observation and inductive generalisation are the only ways in which we reach assurance of matters of fact. Now, if we are prepared to start by accepting these methods as valid, it is permissible to use them reflexively to examine their own procedure. But philosophical unrest proceeds precisely from this, that we are not prepared, without further argument, to accept the testimony of our senses and the validity of inductive generalisations, and are quite prepared to ask why we should not accept as valid forms of deductive reasoning other than those which we normally use. To quell this unrest the Experimental Method by itself is powerless. It holds a mirror before the mind's eye, but does not reconcile us to what we see.

The only other device available to a philosopher is the device which Hume uses, sometimes explicitly and consciously, sometimes without giving notice that he is aware of what he is doing. This device I will call "the Method of Challenge".[1] This method is complementary to the experimental method; by the latter Hume shows how we normally do decide questions of fact, questions of logic, questions of value; if we then demand some further source of knowledge by which we can be assured that these procedures are valid, Hume asks: "What sort of additional knowledge is it that you require? Make or cite a suggestion which has a clear meaning. Are there any conceivable alternative procedures to those which I have described? If you can produce any, I will undertake to convince you that it has manifest inconveniences, with which you would not willingly put up. Moreover, if you think you really distrust the ordinary procedures which I have described, just try and do without them, put your scepticism into practice. I am confident you will fail".

In this way the philosopher *persuades* his customer that

[1]Sometimes, I admit, Hume does not use it when he ought to use it instead of the Experimental Method, as in his arguments for the derivation of every simple idea from a corresponding impression.

he is asking for he knows not what, and induces him to be content with what he has already got. An honest kind of service, not often met with in material commerce, and for which the customer naturally does not feel inclined to pay very much.

The Method of Challenge is a method of persuasion, not of proof. It is persuasion not proof that a man in a state of philosophical perplexity requires, persuasion to accept the first principles of all proofs. This method of persuasion, if successful, opens the way for further employment of the Experimental Method, which is a method of proof. And it is by this method that the philosopher can show us where to find treasures more accessible than the moon we came to ask him for.

The Method of Challenge has reconciled us to accepting our natural condition, and using with humility and confidence the faculties that go with it. Let us turn those faculties where alone the facts can be discovered which will suffice to direct us in the conduct of life; let us turn them on the nature of man in general, and our individual selves in particular, as revealed by experience. Let us study man's behaviour in all conditions, physical, political, social, economic. Let us study the causes and effects of his passions, the way his understanding develops and works, and the sources of his felicity and his misery. Unless we pursue this study we shall never obtain that wisdom of which philosophy is the love, the wisdom that provides a settled and satisfactory way of life.

BIBLIOGRAPHY

J. Y. T. GREIG, *David Hume*, London, 1931.

J. Y. T. GREIG, *The Letters of David Hume*, Oxford, 1932.

R. KLIBANSKY & E. C. MOSSNER, *New Letters of David Hume*, Oxford, 1954.

E. C. MOSSNER, *The Life of David Hume*, Nelson, 1954.

C. W. HENDEL, *Studies in the Philosophy of David Hume*, Princeton, 1925.

B. M. LAING, *David Hume*, London, 1932.

J. LAIRD, *Hume's Philosophy of Human Nature*, Methuen, 1932.

R. W. CHURCH, *Hume's Theory of the Understanding*, 1935.

N. KEMP SMITH, *The Philosophy of David Hume*, Macmillan, 1941.

H. H. PRICE, *Hume's Theory of the External World*, O.U.P., 1940.

J. A. PASSMORE, *Hume's Intentions*, C.U.P., 1952.

A. FLEW, *Hume's Philosophy of Belief*, Routledge & Kegan Paul, 1961.

Part I

HUME'S ACCOUNT OF THE UNDERSTANDING

CHAPTER I

THE DOCTRINE OF IMPRESSIONS AND IDEAS

(Treatise Book I, Part I, Sect. I; Enquiry, Sect. I)

1. *The distinction as drawn by Hume*

THE first part of Hume's Treatise of Human Nature states certain doctrines, apparently of a pyschological kind, which are intended to serve as the first premisses of his system.

The first of these doctrines is that all the contents of consciousness, the perceptions of the human mind, admit of a certain classification, which begins with the distinction between "impressions" and "ideas".

At first sight the distinction seems just, familar and easy. The instances Hume gives are clear. A sensation, such as one of sound, or colour, a feeling such as one of warmth or pain, a passion such as one of rage, are all impressions. A mental image, the sort of perception which represents a sensation or passion in memory or expectation, is an "idea".

But if we ask what is the criterion of this distinction, the matter is not so clear as Hume thought. He says that it consists in the force and vivacity of the "impressions" in contrast to the faintness of the "ideas". That there are difficulties about this is immediately apparent from Hume's own admission that in fever, madness or strong emotion our ideas may approach in vivacity to our impressions, and that sometimes our impressions are so faint and low that we cannot distinguish them from ideas. Such cases Hume apparently regards as rare, abnormal and unimportant. Even if they were, we should still be entitled to ask by what criterion he classifies as an "impression" the perception that is as faint and low as those he calls "ideas". The criterion must be other than that of superior liveliness, which *ex hypothesi* does not apply.

But such cases are not so very rare, and not necessarily abnormal. Suppose you are in a boat at sea, visibility is bad, and you are straining your eyes to pick up a certain buoy in a certain direction. A faint speck appears for a moment in your field of vision; did you see something raised on the top of a distant wave or did you only imagine it? Or suppose you are anxious to know if you are in the process of falling in love with Miss X. A perception occurs of which you ask whether it be a rather vivid representation of the feeling of jealousy of Mr. Y, or that very passion itself in a low degree. How are you to tell which it is?

Now in the case of the visual perception, though this doubt may cause us practical concern on the sea, it does not usually cause us theoretical concern. For we *have* another criterion, though it is not always so easy to use. A visual sensation is caused by light rays striking the retina of the eye and causing certain changes in our nerves and brain. A visual "mental image" is *not* so caused. Its causes are presumed to be either purely psychological, or to be changes within the nervous system, not due in the same direct way to light rays. Similarly with sounds and undulations in the air.

But for philosophical purposes we must notice three things about this way of drawing the distinction.

First it admits by implication that there is no *intrinsic* observable difference, as Hume suggests, between a faint impression and a vivid image. The criterion is based on their causal relationships.

Secondly, it does not apply to the case of passions. Here the nearest analogous distinction depends on the effects of the perceptions. Real jealousy is what makes us behave rudely to Mr. Y, or take considerable trouble to interfere with his enjoyment of Miss X's company. Othello's jealousy was plainly real, judged by its effects on his behaviour, though its causes were imaginary.

Thirdly, this criterion assumes that physical reality is already known. It cannot therefore be used to draw a distinction between sensation and image that will serve for a logical foundation of our beliefs about the physical world. The evidence for the doctrines of the physicist and the physiologist about light rays and nervous discharges consists in the end of sense-experiences of physicists and physiologists, their "observations". And these "observations" must be genuine sensations, "impressions", and not figments of their imaginations. When Hume introduces this distinction as the corner-stone of his theory of Human Knowledge, he presumably means to use it to explain how we obtain our knowledge, or what passes for such, of the physical world. He cannot therefore fall back on this basis for the distinction.[1]

2. *The true basis of the distinction*

The distinction between impressions and ideas, if it is to serve as a basis for a theory of knowledge, is not that between sensation (or passion) and mental image, and it is not that between delusion and reality. Is there any valid distinction which we can suppose Hume to have had in mind, but to have failed to express clearly, which might serve this purpose? I think there is, and we can find it suggested in his own words.

Hume says (Treatise Book I, Part I, Sect. I) "Everyone of himself will readily perceive the difference between feeling and thinking". Feeling, he implies, is having an "impression", thinking is having an "idea". Similarly in the Enquiry (Sect. II, para. 12) he gives "thoughts" and "ideas" as synonyms.

What philosophers have wished to refer to when they use the term "idea" in this way is not, I suggest, primarily mental images, but whatever mental entity is used as a symbol in thinking. Often we use mental images as symbols in our thinking ;

[1] The term "impression" is, in virtue of its philosophical history, loaded with suggestions of this criterion. It was used by medieval philosophers, by the occasionalists, and by Locke to mean the effect produced on our sense-organs or brain by the action of external bodies, whose existence was taken for granted, or for the collateral effect on our consciousness. And this meaning of the term inserts itself at intervals into Hume's thought to the confusion of the reader. For instance, Treatise Book II, Part I, Sect. I. "Impressions of sensation are such as . . . arise in the soul from the constitution of the body, from the animal spirits, or from the application of objects to the external organs", and Treatise Book I, Part I, Sect. II where, he says, more cautiously, that impressions of sensation "arise in the soul originally, from unknown causes".

but often we use other symbols, words seen written, or heard spoken, or felt spoken, or felt as summarily outlined by very incomplete speaking movements of the vocal organs; and often we have mental images which we do not use as symbols in thinking, as in dreaming, day-dreaming, and "imagining that we hear or see" something. In the last sort of case, far from being used as symbols in thinking, they are the very things that we think about, thinking of them, for instance, that they are appearances of real objects.

It is clear, I think, that the distinction Hume really has in mind, and which he requires for his purpose, is that between what we think about, the given, and our thoughts about it, or the symbols by means of which these thoughts are thought. What is given to us to think about we may subsequently classify as a sensation, a passion, an image or even an idea. For we can think about our own thoughts as Hume recognises when he later talks about "ideas of ideas".

In a passage which is particularly relevant to my present point, he says (Treatise Book I, Part III, Sect. VIII), "In thinking of our past thoughts we not only delineate out the objects of which we were thinking, but also conceive the action of the mind in the meditation, that certain *je-ne-sais-quoi*, of which it is impossible to give any definition or description, but which everyone sufficiently understands".

It is clear what Hume's difficulty here is; he has to explain the difference between the idea of my hat, *i.e.*, thinking of my hat, and the idea of my idea of my hat, *i.e.*, thinking of the thought of my hat, as when I remember that I thought of fetching my hat, but did not do so. If the difference between an impression and an idea is solely that of the superior vivacity of one pictorial representation over another, then the idea of my hat and the idea of the idea of my hat must be indistinguishable; each will be a faint picture of a hat. But there is, he now discovers, something else represented in the thought of my thought of my hat, i.e., the act of using an image of a hat to symbolise my hat. In the thought of my hat this is not represented, but actually done. In the thought of my thought of my hat it is represented, but not actually done. What is actually done is

something else; some symbol is used to represent my former
act of using an image of a hat to represent my hat.

To sum up: The distinction which Hume required and for
which he was fumbling in his doctrine of impressions and ideas
is the distinction between the given, or experience,[1] and our
thoughts about the given. In Part I of the Treatise he confused
this distinction with that between sensations and passions on
the one hand, and mental images on the other. The cause of the
confusion was the fact that sensation and passion are the part
of the given about which we most often have to think, and that
images, in most people, are the most common symbols to use
in thinking of them. When he came to reflect on "Ideas of
Ideas" Hume saw that to have an "idea" is not merely to form
a picture; for if it were, an idea and the idea of that idea would
be indistinguishable. He was unable to remedy his account
because he had not seen that thinking consists in the use of
symbols.

3. *The derivation of ideas from experience*

We are now in a position to consider Hume's second
doctrine that every simple idea is derived from a corresponding
impression. The doctrine is stated and professedly proved as
if it was equivalent to "Every simple image is derived from a
corresponding sensation or passion". This proposition is not
clearly intelligible, because the distinction between a simple
and a complex *image* is obscure; and the alleged proofs are
inadequate, consisting merely of suggestions of experiments
which have not in fact been made and would be almost impossible to carry out; moreover there is a suggested experiment
which Hume admits might prove an exception to the general
rule, the experiment of the missing shade of blue.

First as to the division of impressions and ideas into simple
and complex. "Simple perceptions", we are told, "are such as
admit of no distinction nor separation". "The complex are the
contrary of these and may be distinguished into parts". The
instance he gives is that of the particular colour, taste and smell

---

[1] By "experience" Hume means impressions taken collectively. On the view
I am suggesting it must be defined simply as that about which we think,
or could think, as opposed to what we think about it.

of an apple. Individually, each is a simple impression, together they form a complex one, that of the whole apple. Plainly there is some confusion here; the colour, taste and smell of the apple are qualities of it, or if you please of our impression. They are not parts of it. As far as parts are concerned, my impression or idea of an apple, conceived as a picture, may be divided and subdivided into parts almost as long as you please; the only limit being the smallest visual area which I may be capable of perceiving or imagining. It is plainly not such "minima visibilia" (or "imaginabilia") of which Hume is really thinking, as is shown by the instance he takes.

Secondly, let us consider the "experiments" he cites as proofs of the proposition that every simple idea is derived from a corresponding impression. They are, first, "To give a child an idea of scarlet or orange, of sweet or bitter, I present the objects, or in other words, convey to him those impressions; but proceed not so absurdly, as to produce the impressions by exciting the ideas". Secondly, "we cannot form to ourselves a just idea of the taste of a pineapple, without actually tasting it". Thirdly, persons born blind have no ideas of colour, and persons born deaf have no idea of sound.

Now these three observations all seem to be in some sense true. And we feel that there is some important epistemological proposition which they at least illustrate. But it is easy to see that that proposition is not one about *images*. The propositions that no child ever has an orange image before it has seen an orange object, that congenitally blind persons have no images of colour, and that no one has ever formed an image of the taste of a pineapple without actually having tasted one, are psychological propositions for which it would be difficult, if not impossible, to provide adequate empirical proof.

What is hard to doubt is that no child knows what the word "orange" means until it has been shown an orange object and taught to call it "orange". It may, for all we can tell, have had orange images; but it could not possibly have learned that they were "orange" images. Similarly congenitally blind persons may have coloured visual images. But so long as they remain blind, no one can possibly teach them, and no one can suggest how they could learn for themselves, that such experiences are what other people called "coloured images". Finally, even if I should by chance have imagined or dreamed of the taste of a pineapple, until I have eaten a pineapple I cannot know that that dreamed or imagined taste was the taste of a pineapple.

The general proposition which these particular observations illustrate is an epistemological proposition; that to know the meaning of a word or other symbol, our attention must be drawn to some experience, or "given", for which it is by custom or convention used to stand.

Now "To know what the word 'orange' means" may not unnaturally be paraphrased "To know what orange is", and that may not unnaturally be paraphrased "to have the idea of orange". Consequently, our epistemological proposition may not unnaturally be phrased "To have an idea of 'x', I must have experienced 'x' ." This proposition is, I suggest, at least part of what Hume wished to assert when he said that "Every simple idea is derived from a corresponding impression".

We can now see the point of the distinction between simple and complex ideas. The proposition "to have an idea of x, I must have experienced x" is not true without qualification. To take Hume's own example, I have an idea of the New Jerusalem, though I have not seen it. There is another way of learning the meaning of a symbol, besides having one's attention drawn to an instance of the sort of "given" for which it stands. I may learn it by being told its definition. Thus, to take a simple example, I may learn what "awe" means by being told that awe is a combination of fear and respect.

But to learn the meaning of a symbol in this way, I must understand the symbols occurring in the definition. These in turn may be explained by definition, but in the end definitions must work down to symbols whose meaning I have learned "ostensively", i.e., by having my attention drawn to instances of what they stand for.

Here, if anywhere, we shall find what Hume meant by a simple idea. Now it would seem that the meaning of some terms such as "red", "colour", "sound", "smell", etc., can only be learned "ostensively" because they stand for what some philosophers call "simple and unanalysable qualities". Red cannot be represented as any sort of combination of separately illustratable qualities. It is true it is a kind of colour and we can give other examples of colour; but what red is in addition to being a colour, the sort of colour that it is, can only be indicated by exhibiting red objects and contrasting them with objects which are not red. In this sense such terms as "red" may be said to stand for simple ideas.[1] But there are other indefinable terms, whose meaning can only be learned ostensively, which no one would say stand for simple ideas; *e.g.*, "nation", "in love".

Hume should therefore have substituted the distinction between definable and indefinable terms for that between complex and simple ideas. And instead of saying that every simple idea is derived from a corresponding impression, he should have said that every indefinable term can be explained "ostensively", by indicating the sort of experiences to which it refers.

The reason why it is difficult to doubt the truth of this proposition is that it is impossible to think of any other way in which such terms could acquire a meaning, or to produce an instance of a significant term whose meaning cannot be given by definition, and which is not used to refer to experiences of some recognisable sort.

It is really a case of Hume's method of challenge. As he himself says (Enquiry, para. 14), "those who would assert that this proposition is not universally true, have only one and that an easy method of refuting it; by producing that idea which, in their opinion, is not derived from this source. It will then be incumbent on us, if we would maintain our doctrine, to produce

---

[1] A sort of meaning can be attached even to these terms in the other way, by definition or description. For instance, granting that fear is a simple and unanalysable feeling, it would be possible for a person who never felt it or imagined it to learn that "fear" means what other people feel when they are in danger, and the perception of that danger causes them to tremble, go white, etc. Such a person would **in a way** know what "fear" means, but he would not know its full or proper meaning. Philosophers would say that he knew fear "by description" but not "by acquaintance". In Hume's problem of the missing shade of blue, the man is supposed to know the missing shade by description, as the shade intermediate between two shades with which he is acquainted. The unimportant psychological question which Hume asks is simply, could he form an image of the missing shade although he only knew it by description, not by acquaintance? Hume rightly feels that the question is unimportant, but does not see why.

the impression or lively perception which corresponds to it".[1]

I do not think Hume has here propounded his challenge in the most formidable possible way. The sort of argument he envisages might end in a deadlock. Someone might produce for instance the idea of necessary connexion (between a cause and its effect), and allege that this was a simple idea not derived from some given experience, an "a priori", or "innate" idea. Hume would answer by producing the felt customary determination of the mind to pass from the belief in the cause to the expectation of the effect, and say, "that is the impression from which your idea is derived". His opponent might then reply "that is *not* what I mean by causal necessity. The expression plainly has another meaning, but you cannot produce the impression from which it is derived. This shows there *are* innate ideas, of which this is an example".

Hume's only alternative to accepting a deadlock would be to say "what possible grounds have you for saying that the expression has a 'meaning' unless you can either define it or indicate the sort of experience to which it is used to refer? How else have *you* learned a meaning for it, and how do you propose to teach your children its meaning, or ensure that they use the term in the same way as you do?" Or to put it in another and more tiresomely philosophical way "what on earth do you mean by saying it has a meaning? please explain".

The importance of the question has now, by accident as it were, become apparent. On it turns the time-honoured question of innate ideas. From the time of Plato onwards philosophers had maintained that we have ideas not derived from what is given in experience, ideas by means of which we can reason about a reality beyond the reach of experience, the abstract realm of pure mathematical forms, the active substances from which our sense-experiences spring, the spiritual world of immortal souls of which Theology speaks. These ideas, such as unity point, straight line, substance, activity, necessity, spirit, being, they tended to call "innate", meaning that they are a part of the intellectual equipment with which God has endowed us, or in later times "a priori", a more cautious term,

---

[1]Compare Treatise Book I, Part I, Sect. I, p. 13, where the word "challenge" is actually used.

indicating the supposed non-experiential nature of these ideas
without making theological assumptions.

Hume is an empiricist, that is he denies that there are any
such ideas, and asserts that all our ideas are derived from
experience, that we can only think about what is given us in
experience. His doctrine of impressions and ideas is intended
to be a new and incontestable way of putting the empiricist
position.

Finally, I would suggest that it is a mistake to think that
the position I have stated is exclusively concerned with language
in the ordinary sense of public spoken or written symbols.
A man born blind who nevertheless enjoyed visual images
would be unable to converse about them with other people in
any public language. But he might easily be able to think about
them to himself by means of some private symbolism of his
own invention. The same might be true of a mystic and his
mystical experiences. But still it would be true that he could
think of nothing but what was given him in experience to think
about, because he would only be able to think by means of
symbols, and he could only fix the meanings of his symbols by
relating them to certain experiences or types of experience.

ABSTRACT IDEAS

(Treatise Book I, Part I, Sect. VII)

1. *Realism, conceptualism and nominalism*

HUME'S views on abstract ideas do not play such a fundamental part in his system as Berkeley's rather similar views do
in his. But they are interesting as a most forcible and advanced
statement of the nominalist as against the conceptualist
position in the venerable controversy between Realists, Conceptualists and Nominalists about the nature of "Universals".
Not only ink, but blood was shed in the Middle Ages over this
controversy, but I do not propose to go into its history, as it
has no direct bearing on the important parts of Hume's
philosophy. But we must try to understand and estimate the
truth of what Hume says on this subject, as it throws some
light on his conception of the nature of thinking and of ideas.

In the last chapter we concluded that "to have an idea of
x" means to know what the symbol "x" means, *i.e.*, to know
what it is habitually used to stand for. Now, if the symbol
"x" be a proper name, such as "Felix", there is no mystery in
knowing what "Felix" stands for. It stands, say, for a certain
cat with whom we are acquainted.

But let "x" be the general term "cat". What do we know
when we know what "cat" stands for? It does not stand for
any individual cat, nor yet any finite number of actual cats. It
stands, we feel inclined to say, for the whole class of cats, past,
present and to come, wherever, whenever and in whatever
numbers they exist. Or, we may feel inclined to say, it stands

C

for the common nature, "felinity", which is present in all cats and makes us call them all cats.

Now the whole class of cats, past, present and to come, is not a possible object of acquaintance which we can exhibit to others or represent to ourselves in order to fix the meaning of the name. It is some complicated sort of abstraction or figure of speech. To know the class of cats is to know what individuals to classify as cats, and what individuals not to. Or rather, since the individuals which are to be classified as cats are not a finite collection, like the twelve apostles, it is to be able to know of any individual whether it is a cat or not. Now how can we know of any individual that it is a cat, or that it is not a cat?

The realists said that in addition to particular cats, we are aware of another real existence, called the universal cat, or the form of cathood or felinity in general; and that we can tell of any given individual whether it is a cat or not by seeing whether it partakes in this universal, whether the form of cathood is present in it. The universal or form was considered as a real thing, not a figment of the mind, but not a real thing in the sense of a natural object changing and moving in time and space in accordance with the laws of nature. It was regarded as something timeless, unchangeable, intelligible rather than sensible. Cats may come and cats may go but cathood is always one and always the same.

Conceptualists said that this was a gratuitous piece of mythology. They said that you could tell whether any individual was a cat or not, by seeing whether it conformed to the abstract general idea, or concept of cat. The archetype to which an individual must conform to be considered a member of a class, and properly called by a class name, was, according to them, a representation in the mind, a peculiar sort of idea, general in that it applied to all particular cats, abstract in that it represented only the common features of all cats abstracted from, *i.e.*, shorn of, the particular features peculiar to individual cats or certain species of cats.

Now what sort of an idea could this be, and how could we come by it?

The philosopher who, shortly before Hume's time, had

made the most explicit effort to describe an abstract general idea and the process by which we form it was Locke.

Locke had shared Hume's conviction that all our ideas are derived from experience. Even those who did not share this conviction would have to admit that we got such ideas as that of "cat" from experience, whatever might be the case with abstruser ideas. Locke had therefore tried to explain how we got from particular sensations to abstract general ideas. Like Hume he conceived ideas primarily as pictures, images which copied given experiences. Particular ideas would then be copies in the imagination or memory of particular experiences. All experiences were particular. These particular ideas were the material from which abstract general ideas had somehow to be manufactured.

The recipe, according to Locke, was as follows: take a group of particular ideas which are like one another, *e.g.*, a group of ideas of particular cats. Now select one of them, it does not matter which. Get hold of a sort of mental indiarubber and rub out the features of the picture which are not present in the other particular ideas. When you have finished you will be left with a sort of partial, vestigial, highly abstract picture, representing only what is common to all the particular ideas you started with. This is how an abstract idea is made, and it is general because it can be used to stand for anything which corresponds to it, *i.e.*, has those common features, whatever other pecularities it may have.

Now Berkeley had pointed out, and Hume agreed with him, that this recipe was quite impossible to follow, and the supposed resulting picture an absurdity. All cats are coloured (including black, white and grey as colours) and all cats have fur. But some cats are one colour, some another, some have long hair, some have short. Try to eliminate from your mental picture of a sandy cat the sandyness of its colour, and retain the colouredness; try to eliminate the shortness of the fur but retain some representation of furriness, without representing it as either short, long, or medium length fur. Plainly it cannot be done; if you rub out the particular colour, colour in general goes with it; if you rub out the length of the fur, the fur goes with it.

Furthermore, Berkeley and Hume say, there is no need for

these abstract general ideas. Particular ideas serve the purpose
equally well, and are in fact what we use in general thinking.
Locke admits that we start by noticing a certain sort of resemblance between certain particular ideas. It is this resemblance which makes us regard them as all of one class. Therefore
to represent this class, and serve as a criterion for admitting
and rejecting further candidates for admission, it suffices to
take the idea of a particular typical member, and ask of any
candidate whether it has the required resemblance to that
typical member.

Our idea of the typical member, say of the sandy, large,
short-haired, mongrel cat "Felix", will represent him as he is
with all his peculiarities. But in using him as a general symbol
for any cat whatsoever, we ignore his peculiarities, and only
attend to the features in respect of which we require a resemblance in anything to be classified as a cat. And, as Hume
says, we find this causes no inconvenience in our reasoning.

2. Hume's advance on Berkeley's nominalism

Hume's improvements on Berkeley's theory consist in his
emphasis of the role played by customary association and of the
use of many particular images to illustrate the sort of
resemblance required.

The relation between the word and the particular idea, left
undefined by Berkeley, is defined by Hume as a customary
association. The "use" of the particular idea "to stand for" all
other resembling particular ideas, is according to Hume its
power to revive them by association.

In the case of a word with which we are familiar this power
is not usually actually exercised. A single particular image is
evoked and we feel that it has the power to evoke the other
associated ideas if they are needed. One of the purposes[1] for
which they may be needed is illustration. The more numerous
and more varied are the representations of particular cats,
remembered or imagined, actual or possible, that we form and

---

[1]Another purpose is reasoning. The more extensive and varied our gallery
of cat images, the better can we tell what propositions about cats are true,
partly true, and false. An "abstract idea" or "generic image" would not
serve this purpose.

survey, the more clear do we make it to ourselves what we mean by cat, what is or is not a cat, the sort of resemblance we require. The better we are able to do this, the better we understand the meaning of "cat". The process is what is often called "ostensive definition", performed for our own benefit in the imagination.

This view explains how we know *what sort* of resemblance we require between instances of a given kind; it is the sort of resemblance that even the most diverse of the particular cases have to one another. To take Hume's example, a globe of white marble and a cube of white wood are diverse in substance, feel and shape, but alike in colour; together they illustrate the sort of resemblance we require between things that are to be called white.

The merit of this view, if it be tenable, is that it explains, without speculative assumptions, how we can mean something and know what we mean by a general term. To know what "cat" means is not to be aware of some metaphysical or intellectual archetype and know that "cat" is its name, and that "to be a cat" is to conform to or partake in it. It is more a "knowing how to" than a "knowing that", like knowing how to drive a car. It is knowing how to use the word, what to apply it to and what not to apply it to. And just as a man knows how to drive a car if he has acquired certain habits, so a man knows how to use a word if he has acquired certain habits. All that we need to be *acquainted with* is the resemblance between the particular instances, and between the utterances of the associated symbol.

Hume does also suggest that when we hear a word and understand it without reeling off a string of illustrative pictures, it is not only true that we could do so, but we *know* that we could. "The word not being able to revive the idea of all these individuals, only touches the soul, . . . and revives that custom which we have acquired by surveying them. They are not really and, in fact, present to the mind, but only in power . . . (we) keep ourselves in a readiness to survey any of them, as we may be prompted by a present design or necessity".

To attempt an analysis of that state of mind in which we

know that we could do something which we do not actually do would take us too far into the controversial hinterland of Epistemology for the scope of this book. We must be content to admit that it occurs and that its occurrence in this particular form seems to be a necessary part of understanding the meaning of a word, as we understand it when in ordinary discourse someone speaks of an object not present to our senses or memory. It must be admitted it is something of a mystery.

The dangers of the realist and conceptualist views, as seen by the empiricist, are that a realist who thinks he is acquainted with universals will be tempted to regard that acquaintance as a source of knowledge about reality other than and superior to experiment and observation by the senses, while a conceptualist who thinks he has "abstract" ideas, will be tempted to think that they are representations of possible objects. For instance, if a man thinks he has an abstract idea of shape, which just represents shape without colour, warmth, texture, or any sensible quality, he will be tempted to think there may be objects which have only shape and size and no sensible qualities. This according to Berkeley and Hume is nonsense, and according to Berkeley, dangerous nonsense.

Let us then try and summarise Hume's contribution to the problem of universals.

There are two questions to which he suggests answers.

First, what is it that I perceive about two or any finite number of cats that makes me class them together and call them all "cats"? His answer is a certain sort of resemblance between them; *not* some relationship between each of them and some fictitious entity, the eternal form of cathood, or the abstract archetypal concept of cathood in the mind. (Whose mind anyway?)

Secondly, what happens in my mind when I think about cats in general, *i.e.*, when I use the word "cat" not merely to stand indifferently for this or that particular cat, but for *any* cat whatsoever? His answer is that the word "cat" sets a mental custom or disposition in operation, or at least puts it in readiness to operate if required. This disposition is simply our ability to recognise cats when we see them, a disposition to call "cats" only such particulars as resemble the cats we have known in the way they all resemble one another; with it goes an ability to imagine or describe an indefinite number of possible particulars such as we should call " cats" if we met them. It is the feeling of this readiness, consciousness that we have this custom, which makes us say we know what "cat" means or "have the general idea" of cat. It is the association of the word with a custom that gives it its generality, its capacity to stand for "*any*" cat.

His answer to the first question is the same as that of Berkeley; his answer to the second question is an advance on Berkeley's view, in so far as it seeks to clarify the notion of generality, the meaning of "any", by relating it to custom.

Hume's advance on Berkeley may be put thus. The general term "cat" means "any cat". Now a picture of a particular cat, or a set of such pictures, can illustrate what is common to those particular cats, the sort of resemblance they have to one another. It cannot exhibit what we mean by "any". "Any" stands for nothing that is picturable. It is not a feature of the particular objects which make up the real world, though resemblance and difference are. But a custom or power does seem to contain generality in it.

According to this view the term "cat" means "any cat" in the sense of "any cat you like to mention". It means this because it touches off the disposition of the mind to give instances of and recognise instances of cats indefinitely. "Any cat likes milk" is as it were a challenge rather than a statement; it challenges anyone with the necessary mental custom to produce an instance of a cat that does not like milk.

Berkeley had seen that the general and the indeterminate could not be representatively symbolised, but could be symbolised by a conventional symbol. But he did not suggest how this could be done. Hume did.

More extended analysis and criticism of this suggestion of Hume's may be found in a paper by Professor Aaron on "Hume's Theory of Universals" in Proceedings of the Aristotelean Society, and in a Lecture by Professor H. H. Price on "Thinking and Representation" (Henriette Hertz Lecture, British Academy 1946).

CHAPTER III

KNOWLEDGE AND PROBABILITY

(Treatise Book I, Part III, Sect. I; Enquiry, Sect. IV, Part I)

1. *The four kinds of assurance*

H U M E contends that there are only four ways in which we can assure ourselves of the truth of a proposition. First perception by sense or introspection, secondly memory, thirdly deductive demonstration, and fourthly probable reasoning. He has something immensely important to maintain about the last two methods; namely, that deductive demonstrations cannot by themselves prove "matters of fact and existence", and that probable reasonings, which can, are always founded on experience.

The consequence of this doctrine is that no facts about the world can be established by reasoning independently of experience; and that is precisely what metaphysicians of the rationalist school had attempted to do. For instance, Parmenides had professed to prove that there was no void or empty space in the universe, because void is the non-existence of anything, and to assert the existence of non-existence is self-contradictory; and some philosophers, *e.g.*, Descartes, had professed to prove the existence of God on the grounds that God is by definition a perfect being, and non-existence is an imperfection.

It is true that most people are not misled by such sophistries and dismiss them without thought as fine-spun nonsense, just as they dismiss the theory that we have "astral bodies" which, during our sleep, enjoy voyages and adventures on the "astral plane". But it is always possible that some accident of personal influence or unusual experience may lead them to give serious consideration to such nonsense; if they are then unable to say just why it is nonsense, they may quickly find themselves beginning to tend to believe it, or at least admit that there "may be something in it". It is, therefore, not a useless enterprise on the part of philosophers to attempt to show just why and in what sense nonsense is nonsense.

We will now take these four sources of assurance in order.

Hume's views on sense perception are contained in the section of the Treatise called "on Scepticism with regard to the senses". This is one of the most difficult parts of Hume's philosophy, and will be considered in detail later. The general upshot of it is that sight and touch do in fact give us an assurance of the continued and independent existence of bodies. This assurance, though it cannot be rendered wholly satisfactory to our reason or reconciled with the conclusions of natural science, in practice needs no such justification, since no sceptical arguments will ever weaken it; consequently the independent existence of bodies, revealed to us by our senses, is "something we must take for granted in all our reasonings". Anticipating this conclusion Hume takes it for granted in his reasonings concerning knowledge and probability.

The subject of memory is one on which Hume is notoriously weak; but no worse in that respect than other philosophers of his own and earlier times. To remember, according to Hume, consists in having ideas, conceived again as mental pictures. How do these pictures differ from "ideas of the imagination"? Hume mentions two differences.

First (Treatise Book I, Part I, Sect. III) they are more vivid, being intermediate in force and vivacity between an impression and a *mere* idea, or idea of the imagination; secondly (Part III, Sect. V) "Memory preserves the original order and position of its ideas, while the imagination transposes and changes them as it pleases".

By the "original order of the ideas" I take Hume to mean an order the same as that of the impressions from which the ideas are derived. As Hume immediately admits, "this latter difference is not sufficient to . . . make us know the one from the other". For it is only by memory that we can know what the original order of the impressions was. Hume's reference to this difference amounts to no more than saying that by an idea of. memory we mean a true picture of past experiences. The question remains how we distinguish a true picture from a false.

To answer this question Hume can only fall back on the criterion of force and vivacity. If a mental picture lacks the force and vivacity which would mark it as present impression, yet possesses the kind and degree of force and vivacity which constitute belief, and if that belief bears on the face of it some kind of reference to past time, then it is a memory belief; unless, of course, it is a belief about the past reached by inference.

The mysterious "past reference" of an idea of memory is mentioned by Hume in the passage about the memory of a past idea (Treatise Book I, Part III, Sect. VIII); but no attempt at clarification is made. In addition to the mysteriousness of past reference, Hume's whole account of memory is infected with the confusion between mental images and "ideas" considered as the units of thought, and participates in the weakness which this confusion confers on his account of belief in general, which must be considered later.

Let us for the moment content ourselves with saying in Hume's favour, that if he has failed to produce an intelligible account of memory no other philosopher has done so either. And if we accept the familiar fact that in memory we have non-inferential beliefs about our own past experiences, in which we repose a confidence inferior only to our confidence in our present sense perceptions, and which we use along with them as the starting points of our reasoning concerning matters of fact, we are in a position to follow the important contentions which Hume makes about that reasoning.

We come now to Hume's account of "demonstrative reasoning" and its limitations. His position is stated in different ways in the Treatise and in the Enquiry. Let us begin with the Treatise.

We are there told that the relations by the tracing of which reasoning is conducted are resemblance, identity, relations of time and place, proportions in quantity or number, degrees in any quality, contrariety, and causation.

These are divided into two classes, first, such as depend entirely on the ideas which we compare together, and secondly, such as may be changed without any change in the ideas. It is only the former class which are the province of demonstrative reasoning. The members of this class are four, resemblance, contrariety, degrees in quality and proportions in quantity and number.

Causation is, therefore, not an object of demonstrative reasoning, and since causation is the only relation which enables us to make inferences to matters of fact which we do not immediately observe, matters of fact cannot be demonstrated.

Hume then proceeds to enquire how causal relationships are discovered, and answers "from experience"; and how they serve as the basis of factual inferences[1], and answers that the experience of constant conjunction generates a habit of expectation in the mind, the operation of which habit is the inference; we shall have much to say about this later.

2. Relations of ideas and matters of fact

We must now consider the distinction between "Relations of Ideas", relations which depend solely on the ideas compared, and factual relationships, those which may be altered without altering the ideas.

If I endeavour to conceive a triangle whose internal angles together equal more than two right angles, I find I must conceive of something that is not a triangle; that is, if I continue to call it a triangle, I must have altered my idea of a triangle, modified the meaning of the term. For instance, if I call the three-sided figure which consists of two meridians of longitude and a parallel of latitude a triangle, I am allowing figures with curved sides to count as triangles. If, on the other hand, I try to conceive of the moon as being 5,000 miles nearer the earth than it in fact is, I do not have to alter my idea of the moon. That is, in Hume's terminology, spatial relations are not relations of ideas.

Now it is at this point that someone will say, "Such a supposition would amount, for me, to an alteration of my idea

---

[1]By a "factual inference" I mean one whose conclusion is a "matter of fact", not a "relation of ideas".

of the moon. For I am well-informed on astronomical matters, and my idea of the moon is an idea of a body revolving round the earth at a certain distance. All that I believe about the moon becomes a part of my idea of the moon, and I cannot suppose any of those beliefs false without altering my idea of the moon".

Such an objection is difficult to answer, yet we feel that the objector has somehow missed Hume's point, possibly because Hume has not expressed himself correctly. In some way we feel the moon would still be the moon if its orbit shifted closer to the earth, or were discovered to be closer to the earth than we had hitherto supposed. But a rectilinear triangle would no longer be a rectilinear triangle, if its internal angles were not equal to two right angles.

The trouble can perhaps be put this way. People have had a number of different beliefs about the moon, about its size, motion, distance from the earth, etc. Yet they have all called it "the moon", and have meant the same thing by that term. If someone tells me that the moon weighs 100 tons, is made of Cheshire cheese and is about 50 miles from the surface of the earth, I understand his meaning. And it is only on the assumption that he refers to the same thing by the term "the moon" as I do, that I can have a significant argument with him about his views.

When Hume speaks of relations which can be changed without any change in the ideas, he does not mean the private and peculiar ideas of individual persons, the sum total of their beliefs about the object in question. He means the public and common idea of some object or class of objects, which must be known and accepted before any significance can be attached to questions and disputes about that object or class of objects. That is, I suggest, the settled, public habitual meaning of some symbol.

We can now see what is the difference he has in mind. You and I must agree on what we mean by a triangle before we dispute about the sum of its internal angles, and we must agree on what we mean by the moon before we dispute about its distance from the earth. But if I wish to convince you that the internal angles of the triangle are equal to two right angles, I have only to appeal to the agreed meaning of the term "triangle" to show that so long as you stick to that meaning you can't deny the proposition without self-contradiction. But if I wish to convince you that the moon is so many thousand miles away I cannot do it in this manner. I must appeal to some observations or measurements, that is to some experiences of certain astronomers. For no contradiction is involved in the denial of my proposition.

All these difficulties are by-passed by Hume in the Enquiry. He there starts by distinguishing propositions expressing "Relations of Ideas" and propositions expressing "Matters of Fact".[1] The former are discovered by the mere operation of thought, by which we see that the denial involves a contradiction. The latter are not discoverable in this way; the contrary of any matter of fact is still possible, for it involves no contradiction.

There is here no talk about "changing our ideas", and no discussion about what kinds of relationships can be relations of ideas. Hume passes straight from the proposition that matters of fact are not demonstrable, since they involve no contradiction, to the proposition that all reasoning concerning matters of fact seems to be founded on the relation of cause and effect, and thence to the question how relations of cause and effect are discovered.

The conclusion he wishes to reach is that relations of cause and effect are not discovered by demonstration. In the Treatise this is stated as self-evident. "The power, by which an object produces another, is never discoverable from their idea". In the Enquiry it is supported by the following argument :—

Causal relations are the foundations of reasoning about matters of fact.

∴ If causal relations were demonstrable, matters of fact would be demonstrable.

But matters of fact are not demonstrable.

---

[1] There is an unfortunate ambiguity in Hume's use of this phrase, which causes some obscurity in his account of empirical reasoning. He uses it to mean both (a) a proposition whose contradictory is intelligible (a synthetic proposition) and (b) a proposition which asserts the existence of some object (an existential proposition). It is true that all existential propositions are synthetic, but the converse is false. e.g., there are synthetic hypothetical propositions which are not existential.

∴ Causal relations are not demonstrable.

From this point the argument is much the same in the two works.

3. *A priori and empirical propositions*

The distinction between relations of ideas and matters of fact is supremely important. Propositions asserting "relations of ideas", whose opposites are self-contradictory, have become known as "analytic propositions". Those of which this is not true, factual propositions, have been named "synthetic". Propositions that can be ascertained without appeal to experience are called "*a priori*", those that can only be ascertained from experience "empirical". Hume's contention is that no *a priori* propositions are synthetic, all *a priori* propositions are analytic, all synthetic propositions empirical.

This contention has become the corner-stone of modern empiricism, and its chief weapon against rationalistic metaphysics. In practical life it is often of the last importance to be sure whether a proposition asserts a relation of ideas or a matter of fact; muddle-headed and unscrupulous persons frequently attempt to prove matters of fact by producing unanswerable truisms that really only assert relations of ideas.

Some time ago the governing body of an Oxford College was debating whether or not to insure its pictures, many of which were old masters. The philosophy tutor, who for one reason or another was against the proposal, produced the following argument. "Insurance is an arrangement for the replacement of the articles insured in case of loss; these pictures are irreplaceable, therefore they cannot be insured." No one could answer this, but commonsense prevailed, and the pictures were insured.

Now if, persuaded of Hume's principles, we examine this argument, we see that it merely asserts a relation of ideas, a logical connexion between the ideas of insurance and replacement. All that can follow from this is that the contract into which it was proposed that the College should enter with the

Insurance Company was not properly speaking an insurance. The argument does nothing to decide whether the proposed contract would be advantageous to the College or not.[1]

---

[1] A beautifully explicit instance of this fallacy is contained in a statement by the French Communist M. Maurice Thorez, published in *The Times*, February 23rd, 1949. "First, the Soviet Union, the fatherland of Socialism, cannot, by definition, practise a policy of aggression and war, which is the characteristic of imperialist powers. Secondly, the Communist position is based on facts, not on hypothesis. . . ."

CHAPTER IV

CAUSALITY

(Treatise Book I, Part III, Sects. II-VI)

1. *Factual inferences and causal relations*

As we saw in the last chapter, the relation of cause and effect is of interest to Hume principally because he regards it as the foundation of all factual reasoning. So far we have noted without comment Hume's premiss that all inferences to matters of fact not actually observed depend on the relation of cause and effect. We must now ask what justification this premiss has.

Hume himself considers the question in Section II of Part III of the Treatise. His argument is as follows.

"All kinds of reasoning consist in nothing but a comparison, and a discovery of those relations, either constant or inconstant, which two or more objects bear to each other". Now there are three possible cases. (a) Where none of the objects is present to our senses. In this case we can compare only our ideas of them, and the most that can result is the demonstration of a relation of ideas, an analytic proposition. (b) When all the objects are present to our senses. In that case we can arrive at a synthetic proposition, but we do so by perception, not by inference. We perceive a similarity or a spatial or temporal juxtaposition of objects. (c) Where some of the objects are present to our senses and the others are not. Given a certain smell, for instance, I can infer that bacon and eggs are being cooked. In this case I "discover" (we are told later how) the causal relation between the smell which I perceive and bacon and eggs which I don't perceive, and from the smell plus this relation I infer the existence of the other term of the relation.

Now Hume says the relation of cause and effect is the only relation in which an observed object can be "discovered" to stand to an unobserved object, whose existence can thus be inferred.

The justification of this contention is really a challenge; show me a factual inference from an observed to an unobserved object founded on a relation which is not either itself a causal relation, or known as the conclusion of some previous causal inference. All the cases which we at first feel inclined to adduce fail to meet this challenge. We might say, for instance, that from the *identity* of the chair I now see with that on which I sat yesterday I can infer that it will carry my weight. But, Hume says, (a) how do you know that it *is* the same chair? Only by reasoning that if another but similar chair had been substituted for it, you would have observed certain effects which you do not observe; and (b) how do you know that because the chair supported you yesterday it will support you to-day? Only because you know that the chair, in virtue of the shape, size, consistency, etc., which it still possesses, is capable of supporting your weight; *i.e.*, that the *result* of your sitting down on it will be rest and not continued motion towards the centre of the earth.

Again, from a photograph, you may infer the existence of an object resembling it. But only because you know how photographs are *produced*.

In general, whenever we can say of a given object x, that it must be related in a certain way, other than a causal way, to an object y which is not given, we must justify ourselves by saying *why* it should be so related. And the answer to such a "why?" will always turn out to be some statement about causes and effects. This is Hume's ground for saying that all factual inferences are founded on the relation of cause and effect.

The question remains to be answered, how do we discover causal relations? Hume's answer to this emerges from the discussion of the idea of cause which follows.

2. *The relation of Cause and Effect* (Treatise Book I, Part III, Sect. II)

Hume's task is to examine the idea of cause by searching for the impression or impressions from which it is derived. For what given elements of experience is the term "cause" used as a symbol ? A *prima facie* analysis of the idea of cause is given which sets the main problem for the remainder of Part III.

"Let us therefore cast our eyes", he says, "on any two objects which we call cause and effect, and turn them on all sides in order to find that impression which produces an idea of such prodigious consequence".

He first notes that no *quality* of any object which we consider a cause can be the origin of the idea. For there is no discoverable quality which is common to all objects, but all objects, we suppose, have their effects. It must therefore be some *relation* among objects.

Hume then states what are the relations which are always either discovered, or, where not discovered, presumed to exist, between objects which we call causes and effects. It is necessary to add the qualification about presumed existence, because all that Hume purposes to do at present is to analyse the common idea of cause and effect, though that idea may be somewhat erroneous. The relations which he discovers are priority in time (the cause prior to the effect), contiguity in time and place, and necessary connexion.

Now plainly it is the necessary connexion which is the essential element in the idea. It is the necessary connexion between a cause and its effect which justifies us in inferring from the one to the other, and whose presence we express by saying that given (a) the cause, the effect (b) *must* attend it.

The question whether spatial and temporal contiguity and priority in time are indispensible elements in the idea is therefore of secondary importance. Thus he says of spatial contiguity, "We may suppose it such (*i.e.*, an essential part of the idea of a cause), according to the general opinion, till we find a more proper occasion to clear up this matter, by examining what objects are or are not susceptible of juxtaposition and conjunction". The occasion is found in Part IV, Section V, where he points out that sounds and smells, passions and volitions cannot properly be said to have shapes or positions at all, but do enter into causal relationships. It is not, therefore his final opinion that spatial contiguity is an essential part of the idea of causation.

The question of the time relation between cause and effect

he never clears up. He gives what purports to be an argument to show that effect must follow cause in time. But he declines to say whether he finds the argument satisfactory, and dismisses the affair as of no great importance.

The argument is really one side of a troublesome little dilemma, which may be stated as follows: Either all effects come into existence at the same moment as their true causes, in which case the whole chain of causes and effects which make up the history of the world must be telescoped into a single instant; or else some causes exist for a finite time without being attended by their effects, in which case they cannot be true causes; they must be awaiting the concurrence of some other condition which is necessary to render them effective.

Now it is important in itself to solve this dilemma, though it is true that the question of the temporal relation between cause and effect is irrelevant to Hume's argument, which is concerned only with the necessary connexion, which alone renders the inference possible. The dilemma does show that it is unsatisfactory to think of a cause as Kant, for instance, defines it, as an event on which another event *follows* according to a rule.

Although this is how we think of it for many purposes in daily life, and in the early stages of scientific investigation, it is not the sort of connexion which advanced sciences seek to establish. It you look up the laws in text books of physics and chemistry, you will find that they do not tell you that if one sort of event occurs, another sort of event will follow. They state equations, or relations of functional dependence of one measurable quantity on another.

A simple example is provided by the law which Archimedes discovered in his bath. This is usually stated "A body immersed in water loses in weight the weight of the water displaced". Now if this meant that the event of the immersion of a body is followed by a loss in weight equal to that of the water it has displaced, we should be immediately entitled to ask, does the loss in weight take place instantaneously, immediately after the immersion, or is there a time lag, during which the weight so to speak evaporates? But it does not mean this. It means that, at any moment you like to choose, the difference between the weight the body had or would have in air, and the weight it has or would have immersed in water, is equal to the weight of the water displaced, if and when it is displaced. It states an equation of the simple form $x-y=z$, by means of which, given any two of the terms, you can infer the third.

But, although the law refers to any moment you like to choose, the operation of the law does not tend to reduce the chain of events to a point instant. The immersion of a body in water is a process which takes time, and it can remain immersed as long as you please. But at any moment during that time its weight is the difference between its unimmersed weight and the weight of the water displaced.

Hume, then, was right in dismissing spatial and temporal contiguity and temporal priority of cause to effect as unimportant elements in the popular notion of causation. What is common both to the popular vague notion and to the scientific notion is the "necessary connexion". Connexion need mean nothing more than some relationship or other, whatever relationship is expressed by the scientist's equation. It is rarely if ever simple temporal sequence. But it must be in some sense "necessary"; it must be reliable, constant not only in the observed instances, but in the unobserved case which we wish to predict; otherwise inference is impossible, where questions of fact are concerned.

Accordingly, he proceeds again to examine any case of causal connexion, in order to see wherein its necessity lies. What is the impression from which this idea of necessity is derived? Again it is no quality of the objects. Survey your body immersed in the bath as long as you please; you will not perceive in it, or in the water, any necessity of losing weight. Nor is it any relation between the objects. The body is immersed in the water, the loss of weight is equal to the weight of the water displaced. But necessity is neither immersion nor equality. We appear to have come to a dead end.

Hume, however, does not despair. Elsewhere he remarks, "there cannot be two passions more nearly resembling one another than philosophy and hunting".[1] So he takes a leaf from the hunter's book and proceeds to "beat about the

[1]Treatise Book II, Part III, Sect. X.

neighbouring fields" in the hope of hitting off the quarry, which he has failed to find where he first expected it.

The "neighbouring fields" are two connected questions, first "for what reason we pronounce it necessary that everything whose existence has a beginning, should also have a cause", and secondly, "why we conclude that such particular causes must necessarily have such particular effects; and what is the nature of that inference we draw from the one to the other, and of the belief we repose in it".

I must pause at this point to emphasize the momentous nature of the hunt on which Hume is engaged; and since the hunt develops into a long and very intricate operation I will try to provide the reader in advance with a summary plan in order to help him in following it.

The quarry is the source of the idea of necessity; that idea is the foundation of all our reasoning concerning matters of fact, that is of the whole of history, geography, cosmology, and all the natural sciences. On it is built our whole conception of what is to be found on the surface of the earth, beneath it, and in space around it; of the laws of nature according to which things happen, of the historical processes by which all things arrived at their present state, and of what may be expected to happen in the future. Unless this foundation is sound, unless the reasoning based on it can in some sense be called rational, the whole edifice is a mere fantasy.

Now for a summary of the operation.

It is first shown that neither the proposition that every event must have a cause, nor the proposition that any given event is the effect of any given other event, is intuitively or demonstrably evident. We have no power of penetrating into the concealed essences of things and seeing that one object necessarily implies another. It is only where we have experience of constant conjunction, as in the case of flame and heat, that we pronounce one event the cause of another; nor do we require anything else. It is only because nature reveals more and more regularity the more closely we are able to investigate her that we believe every event to have a cause (Treatise Book I, Part III, Sect. XII). If closer investigation revealed only more and more randomness, we should not believe in the reign of universal law.

Hume then points out that what the experience of constant conjunction between flame and heat makes us do, is to expect heat when we see flame, in other words infer heat from flame. When we are prepared to do this, we say flame causes heat, or is *necessarily* attended by it. What we *mean* then by saying that flame and heat are necessarily connected is that we are disposed to infer the one from the other; we simply *express* the felt constraint of habit compelling us to pass from the perception of the flame to the belief in the heat.

Closely interwoven with the progress to this conclusion is an account of the nature of belief. This, Hume says, consists in that felt force or vivacity of an idea, which nothing but customary association with a present impression can give.

Finally, developing out of his account of belief, there is a discussion of the difference between genuine belief and certain other states of mind which simulate it, the illusions of poetry, drama and fiction for instance, and of the difference between rational or probable beliefs, adequately supported by experience, and irrational beliefs based merely on education, prejudice or hasty generalisations. We all do, he admits, form such irrational beliefs under the influence of various emotional causes; but no one, on reflection in a cool hour, expects such beliefs to be verified or gives settled and habitual credence to anything but the evidence of experience.

If the reader feels that he is not likely to be entirely satisfied with this as a justification of factual reasoning, he has my sympathy; but let him wait to hear what can be said in Hume's defence when we consider his arguments in detail.

3. *Our conviction that every event has a cause* (Treatise Book I, Part III, Sect. III)

Hume gives refutations of various *a priori* arguments by which philosophers have professed to demonstrate that every event has a cause. He has little difficulty in showing that they all beg the question. No reformulations can render these refutations more convincing, and they seem to me to be open to no objections; I therefore refer the reader to Hume's own words; if they do not convince him, I cannot.

At the end of the section Hume concludes that, since the proposition that every event has a cause is not intuitively or demonstratively certain, our belief in it must arise from observation and experience; but instead of going on to consider how it arises from observation and experience he says that he prefers to "sink this question in the following, 'Why we conclude that such particular causes must necessarily have such particular effects, and why we form an inference from one to another' ". He holds out the promise that "It will, perhaps, be found in the end, that the same answer will serve for both questions".

Now this promise is never explicitly redeemed, and it is not common to find in students of Hume a clear understanding of how Hume thought we become assured of the proposition that every event has a cause. I will therefore cease, for a moment, to follow Hume step by step in his hunt for necessity, in order to save the reader the trouble of himself hunting for Hume's answer to this question.

His answer is given, I think, in the section on the probability of causes (Treatise Book I, Part III, Sect. XII), and in the Enquiry, para. 67, in the section on liberty and necessity. In each of these passages, which are practically identical, Hume is explaining why "philosophers", by which he means not only philosophers but also natural scientists, do not believe in chance, though the vulgar often do. Now to disbelieve in fortuitous events is equivalent to believing that every event has a cause. Here, then, Hume is telling us how experience and observation give rise to the opinion that every event has a cause.

The vulgar, according to Hume, only succeed in finding approximate regularities in the course of their experience. Certain medicines usually cure certain diseases; sometimes they fail; that's a bit of bad luck. Most clocks usually keep time; this one has not today; bad luck. They are content still to talk of cause and effect, but to suppose that causes sometimes fail to produce their due effects, just misfire as it were, "though they meet with no impediment in their operation".

But "philosophers" observe that nature is much more complex than appears at first sight; it contains elements that elude our everyday observations by their minuteness or remoteness. They therefore see that it is at least possible that the irregularities may proceed not from chance, but from concealed counteracting causes. This possibility is converted into certainty by the further observation that whenever an exact scrutiny can be made, the counteracting cause can always be discovered. Consequently, they form a "maxim" that the connexion between all causes and effects is equally necessary, and that its seeming uncertainty in some instances proceeds from the secret operation of contrary causes. That, apart from the illustration of the watch with a bit of dust in it, is all he says.

Now first let us observe that he is here, in effect, arguing for the proposition that every event has a cause. It might be thought that he is merely arguing that all causes are certain in their operation, and not merely approximately certain. But if we were to admit that a cause "misfired", and there was no counteracting cause, no explanation of the misfire, this would be tantamount to admitting that the misfire was an uncaused event. The causal relation is a relation of necessary connexion, as Hume says, and chance is the opposite of necessity.

Secondly, we must admit that if Hume were speaking today, he would be overstating his case. It is not true that whenever an exact scrutiny is possible, the cause is found. We have not yet discovered the cause of cancer, though we have as good opportunities for observing cases of cancer and the conditions under which they occur, as we have of observing any other disease. But we can say that in general our success in discovering regularities, relations of exact and unvarying dependence, is roughly proportionate to the minuteness and extent of the observations that we can make. This, of itself, would be sufficient to justify the formation of a "maxim" that there are always exact laws to be found. Where minute investigation fails to disclose them, it always remains possible that agencies still exist which our instruments cannot detect, and the triumphant progress of science in a variety of fields renders it highly probable.

There is, however, one instance in which modern scientists claim to have reason for supposing that there is a real uncertainty in the nature of things; that is in the behaviour of individual protons and electrons. According to the "Uncertainty Principle" of Heisenberg, the ultimate laws of physics are merely statistical; there is a randomness in the actual behaviour of individual particles. But the randomness of their behaviour is limited by statistical laws in such a way that the large collections of particles which form the bodies studied by sciences other than subatomic physics behave quite regularly. In this instance some scientists say that it is in principle impossible that minuter observations could be made, and meaningless to suppose that unobservable agencies are at work.

Nevertheless, even if Hume thinks that the empirical evidence that justifies this maxim is better than a modern scientist would admit it to be, most modern scientists would agree that it is an empirical question whether all events in nature obey regular laws, and, if so, whether the laws are statistical or exact. And I think they would approve of his calling it a "maxim".

Thirdly, while agreeing with Hume's account of the way in which the conviction that every event has a cause is to be justified, I am doubtful about his account of its origin.

The "vulgar" of whom Hume speaks seem to be singularly unsuperstitious. There is considerable evidence that even in Hume's time in England, if a peasant's cow died from no discoverable cause, and, in spite of having the best of food and attention, the peasant did not ascribe the event to chance; he was more likely to ascribe it to the influence of the "evil eye" of some malicious neighbour, or the operations of a witch. The possibility of secret agencies being at work is only too apt to present itself to the unphilosophical mind; such minds entertain the darkest suspicions about the hidden springs and secret principles of nature. The "philosopher's" suspicions differ in that they are less dark; he sees that there is no need to suppose that the secret principles at work are purposive principles similar to those which regulate voluntary human behaviour, and discovers good evidence to suppose that they are usually of another kind.

It may well be that there is a natural instinctive tendency to suspect the existence of some cause of every event; and that this instinct at first lends force to the belief in magic and spirits, and later, as a result of wider experience, to the belief in the universal reign of natural law.

Finally, it is necessary to forestall a possible objection; a reader who has read some philosophy may object that Hume is here saying (which he is) that the proposition that every event has a cause is arrived at by induction, and that this cannot be true, because the proposition expresses a necessary pre-supposition of all induction.

This objection is mistaken. What is presupposed in all induction (the "presumption on which all probable reasoning rests" as Hume calls it) is that the unobserved will resemble the observed. This principle is ultimate and cannot be a conclusion of probable reasoning, as Hume himself points out (Treatise Book I, Part III, Sect. VI). This principle could lead us to infer from experience either that nature is capricious and irregular, or that it is regular and obeys laws. If no regularity could be found in our experience, we should conclude that all nature was irregular; the principle of probability would then be of no *further* use to us; the only prediction it would enable us to make would be that no predictions could be relied upon.

Fortunately, we find a regularity roughly proportionate to the extent and minuteness of the observations which we can make. We therefore infer, according to the principle, that were we able to observe everything adequately we should find everywhere a complete regularity, and that this regularity of the observed would be found to extend to the unobserved future. Having thus established the regularity of nature we can then proceed to make further detailed predictions in accordance with the principle of probability.

It is therefore true that unless nature were regular we should be unable to make any particular predictions by induction; induction would have no use. But it would not be invalid; on the contrary it would have established that very fact, the capriciousness of nature, which precluded its further application.

4. *Our beliefs in specific causal connexions* (Treatise Book I, Part III, Sect. VI)

Let us now turn to Hume's discussion of the second question, the answer to which he hopes will throw light both on the question why a cause is always thought to be necessary for every event, and on the idea of necessary connexion. This question is, why we think certain specific events to be causally connected, and what is the nature of the inference we make from the one to the other, for instance from flame to heat.

Now inference, according to Hume, consists in passing

from one belief, or set of beliefs, to another. For such a process
to take place, there must be a belief or beliefs which precede,
and are independent of, the inference. These original uninferred
beliefs, if the inference is to conclude in a belief about a matter
of fact, must be either impressions of the senses (or of reflection)
or ideas of memory. As we have seen, what distinguishes both
impressions and ideas of memory from mere ideas, is, according
to him, merely their superior force, vivacity, firmness, solidity,
or whatever you like to call it. They feel different. And this
felt difference is our assent or belief. (Treatise Part III,
Sect. V.)

The question of the nature of factual inference is therefore
how and under what conditions is this vivacity extended from
an impression or memory to an idea, so that that idea becomes
a belief, a conclusion of inference. It has been agreed that this
only happens where we can "trace a relation of cause and
effect". But we do not yet know what this relation is. Its nature,
and our means of discovering it, will, Hume hopes, come to
light if we consider in what circumstances we actually do make
such inferences, and just what happens in our mind when we
do it. For instance, I see a flame and thereupon expect heat.
Why? Because the two are necessarily connected. This answer
has been found to be insufficiently clear. Therefore, Hume asks,
just what is there about flame, in the absence of which I should
not have expected heat when I saw a flame?

Section VI of Part III of the Treatise opens with a paragraph
in which Hume in a succession of memorable sentences tells
what is *not* the answer to this question. It is not, he says, that
we penetrate into the essence of flame, and see that flame, of
its essential nature, *implies* heat.

> " There is no object which implies the existence of any
> other, if we consider these objects in themselves, and never
> look beyond the ideas which we form of them. Such an
> inference would amount to knowledge (*i.e.*, demon-
> strative or intuitive knowledge like that of mathematics)
> and would imply the absolute contradiction and impossi-
> bility of conceiving anything different. But as all distinct
> ideas are separable, it is evident there can be no
> impossibility of that kind. When we pass from a present
> impression to the idea of any object, we might possibly

have separated the idea from the impression, and have substituted any other idea in its room".

For instance, I can quite easily conceive or imagine a flame that froze me instead of burning me. I can write an intelligible fairy story in which a magician brings it about that a certain fire has this effect.

It is not necessary to discuss here whether Hume thought that it was *practically* impossible to discover the real essences of things, either because of the deficiencies of our microscopes (as Locke thought) or because of the limitations of our faculties (as Kant thought), or whether he thought that it was *logically* impossible because all talk of real essences was meaningless. His point is simply that we do not in fact need to make any penetration into the real essences of things when we discover causal connexions. The discovery is not derived from any such penetration. Without bothering to try to penetrate into the essence of flame, perfectly unscientific people consider it a cause of heat and expect it to burn them. They do it, as Hume says, "without further ceremony". They do not consult physicists or metaphysicians. And what makes them do it, Hume asks? It is experience. And what form does the experience take that makes them do it? We all know the answer to this one too. It is the experience of a constant conjunction between flame and heat in the past that makes us call the one cause and other effect, without any further ceremony.

We must note here that Hume goes a little further than saying it is past experience of the constant conjunction; he says it is memory of the conjunctions in the past. This does not seem to be always true, as he recognises later in the same chapter, when he speaks of the automatic association between a word and the idea it signifies. Our past experiences often determine our present expectations even when we do not, and perhaps cannot, recall the particular past experiences which are relevant.

This phenomenon is particularly noticeable in cases where the experiences of past conjunctions are many and complex, but all contribute to determine a single decision. It is from a wide range of past experience of warfare, and possibly of other things, that the brilliant commander knows, in the heat of battle, the exact moment to launch the decisive cavalry charge; if you asked him to recite those past experiences, he very probably could not do so. We have a name, a rather misleading name, for the capacity to do this sort of thing successfully. We call it "intuition".

Hume has thus discovered another feature of a typical case of cause and effect, beside the temporal and spatial relations of the two events. It is the constancy of these two relationships in cases of similar events in the past. And although it is this new feature which, in fact, makes all the difference and is the sufficient condition of our calling them cause and effect, he has not yet solved his problem.

He wants to find the origin of that idea of necessary connexion, which serves as the basis of inferences. The constant conjunction cannot by itself be the origin of this idea. If one case of flame followed by heat cannot give rise to an idea of necessary connexion, then how can seven cases of the same thing do it? We are only "multiplying, not enlarging the objects of our mind". But "It would be folly to despair too soon".

He decides, therefore, to continue the examination of the nature of that inference, which we do in fact make, whenever we have experience of constant conjunction; in this way he hopes to throw further light on the idea of that necessary connexion which we regard as the foundation of such an inference; and, prophetically, he says "Perhaps it will appear in the end, that the necessary connexion depends on the inference, instead of the inference's depending on the necessary connexion". In philosophy, it is frequently found that if the positions of the cart and the horse are reversed, the equipage goes all the better.

Now an inference of the kind in question consists at least in what Hume calls a "transition" from an impression or memory of one object to the idea of another which we call its cause or effect. I see a flame and pass to the idea of heat; and we have seen that it is experience of constant conjunction that makes me do so. Now Hume asks, does that experience produce that transition by means of any chain of reasoning? We have already seen that reason can discover no essential connexion, no direct logical implication between flame and heat. He now asks, can reason find an indirect logical connexion, in which the experience of past conjunctions serves as a link?

He considers and refutes two forms which this indirect reasoning might be supposed to take; and challenges anyone to produce any other suggestions ("I desire that this reasoning may be produced").

The first form which he suggests that the reasoning might take is as follows:

> Unobserved instances must resemble observed instances.
>
> Observed instances of flame have been accompanied by heat.
>
> ∴ Unobserved instances of flame will also be accompanied by heat.

Of this reasoning, Hume asks how we arrive at the first premiss. It is not an analytic proposition, whose contradictory is inconceivable. A change in the course of nature is perfectly conceivable. On the contrary it states a matter of fact about the universe which might conceivably not have been the case. It can, therefore, only be established, if at all, by probable reasoning from experience. But this is exactly the sort of reasoning for which it is always required, according to the present suggestion, as a first premiss; it cannot, therefore, be established by probable reasoning without a glaring *petitio principii*. Hume puts this epigrammatically, but not very accurately, by saying, "The same principle cannot be both the cause and the effect of another".

Hume does not deny that the uniformity of nature is the "presumption" on which all probable reasoning is founded. His point is that it is merely a presumption, which cannot be proved. He also points out later (Section VIII) that it is usually merely a tacit presumption, not an explicit premiss. We do, as a matter of fact, make it, and when our inferences proceed in accordance with it we call them "reasonable", in the sense of probable, and trust them. To distrust them, although we saw them to be made in accordance with this presumption, because we could not prove the truth of the presumption, would be a form of scepticism which Hume challenges anyone to put into practice.

The second form which it might be suggested the reasoning takes, is more or less that suggested by Locke. It is as follows:

> The constant conjunction of heat with flame implies a power in flame to produce heat.
>
> If flame has a power to produce heat, it must always produce it.

The suggestion here is that, although we cannot, as Locke had admitted, "penetrate" into the real essences of things and observe their powers, yet from the constant conjunction of appearances we can *infer* something about those real essences, *i.e.*, their powers of producing other things known to us by their characteristic appearances. It is the inferred power of whatever is the real nature of flame to produce whatever may be the real nature of what we call heat, that is supposed to form the basis of the inference from flame to heat.

Hume in answer says that he will refrain from pointing out that the ideas of "power" and "production" are really identical with that of causation, for the source of which we are searching. He grants, for the sake of argument, that the conjunction of the appearances we call heat with the appearances we call flame in certain observed cases, proves that in *those* cases, at *those* times, the real natures behind the appearances of flame had a power to produce the real natures behind the appearances of heat. But, he asks, how can you tell that behind a new appearance of flame lies a similar real nature with a similar power? And how can you tell that the real nature behind any given appearance of flame will continue to possess such a power one moment after you have ceased to observe the accompanying appearance of heat?

Without an appeal to the presumption of the uniformity of nature, which he has already shown to be non-rational, we "can never prove, that the same power must continue in the same object or collection of sensible qualities; much less that a like power is always conjoined with like sensible qualities".

This argument of Hume's seems to me to be of the greatest importance; it could perfectly well be restated to meet an opponent who thought that we really could perceive powers in real things, not merely infer them from sensible appearances; for instance Professor Stout.[1]

---

[1] "Mind and Matter", Book I, Chapter II.

Even if we can perceive or feel in the bow we bend a power or active tendency to straighten itself and propel the arrow, how do we know that other bows of similar material will have similar powers, or that this bow will continue to possess this power after we have ceased to feel it? The idea of "power" or "active tendency" is not the essential element in our idea of a cause; it is not the same as that idea of *general* necessary connexion which we need to justify causal inferences. What we need to know is that bows as such will straighten, not merely that this bow is now felt or inferred to be exerting a power of pulling at our hand.

Hume concludes that the experience of constant conjunction does not provide a logical link which enables us to make causal inferences by demonstrative reasoning. Yet it is what somehow enables us to make such inferences. Hume says that the only possible explanation is that it facilitates the transition from the impression or memory to the idea by setting up an association in the imagination.

Fancy, Hume admits, is free as the wind; "Thought . . . may leap from the heavens to the earth, from one end of the creation to the other, without any certain method or order". Alternately, one "may fix his attention during some time on any one object without looking further". But sometimes a discoverable principle is at work guiding the sequence of our ideas; this principle is association; and the relations between impressions which give rise to a tendency to association between their corresponding ideas are resemblance, contiguity in time or place, and causation.

There is thus no difficulty in seeing how repeated contiguity of similar impressions gives rise to a strong associative link between the corresponding ideas, and a tendency to pass from the one to the other. The flame I see revives the ideas of past flames which resembled it; these were all spatially and temporally contiguous with heat, and their ideas, therefore, introduce the idea of heat. Had half of them been attended by cold instead, the idea of cold would also have been introduced, and I should not have known what to expect. As it is, the idea of heat holds the field. It soon happens that the mediating ideas of the past instances of flame drop out of the mental process, and the impression of a flame evokes the idea of heat

E

immediately. The two ideas are then, in Hume's terminology, associated by the relation of cause and effect. It is this automatic association which enables us to "reason" on the relation of cause and effect.

Now the cat is really out of the bag, or to continue Hume's hunting metaphor, the quarry is well started and driven into the open. We can see what species of animal it is, and Hume could well have told us; but he prefers first to make very sure of catching it. Nevertheless, we will anticipate the final kill and post-mortem examination.

The necessary connexion is that relation between a cause and its effect which enables us to infer the one from the other, and makes us feel justified in doing so.

Hume has described the conditions under which we make such inferences and feel justified in doing so; when the constant conjunction of like objects in the past has made us associate the idea of the one with that of the other. These conditions are the foundation of the inference, therefore they must be the necessary connexion.

Hume puts the argument with admirable conciseness in the section on Necessary Connexion (Treatise, p. 163). "The necessary connexion betwixt causes and effects is the foundation of our inference from one to the other. The foundation of our inference is the transition arising from the accustomed union. These, therefore, are the same". Necessity is in the mind of the inferrer, just as beauty is in the eye of the beholder and virtue in the mind of the approver, as Hume later maintained.

But Hume is not yet quite ready to make this final revelation. He has not yet completed his account of inference; for inference is a transition not merely from one *idea* to another, but from one *belief* to another, and so far he has only thrown out suggestions as to the nature of belief, suggestions which require further elaboration.

He wants to distinguish belief from similar but different states of mind; and, since he has maintained that the causal relation is the sole foundation of all factual reasoning, he wants to distinguish rational beliefs from irrational beliefs, and show that the former are identical with beliefs inferred in accordance with an association due to constant conjunction in past experience. Finally, to bring the whole argument in line with his doctrine of impressions and ideas, he wants to show that belief and inference are a matter of feeling, and make clear just what is that feeling which we get when we infer an "effect" from its "cause", and which is the impression from which the idea of necessary connexion is derived.

CHAPTER V

BELIEF

1. *The Nature and Causes of Belief* (Treatise Book I, Part III, Sects. VII, VIII, X, and Appendix; Enquiry, paras. 39-45)

Hume points out that he is here treating a subject of whose importance and difficulty previous philosophers had been unaware, and on which they had thrown no light; he says that he finds it very difficult, and that even when he thinks he understands it, he has the greatest difficulty in finding terms to express his meaning. (Treatise, p. 99.)

Recollection of these statements should temper our criticisms of his views; it has not always tempered the observations of his critics. Too often a critic just takes his formal definition of a belief as a lively idea associated with a present impression and points out that it does not square with the facts. It is surely fairer to consider all that he says on the subject, to ponder on its implications, to consider the relations of those implications to his views on other topics, for instance on abstract ideas, and see if that "understanding" of the question which he found it so difficult to express was not really something like the truth.

Hume's first concern in Section VII is to point out how the nature of the problem had been hitherto concealed by the defective traditional account of judgement as "the separating or uniting of different ideas" (footnote, p. 98).

This account, he holds, is false. When another person believes a proposition which I do not believe, *e.g.*, "Cæsar died in his bed", we both unite the same ideas, and form the same conception or complex idea of Cæsar dying in his bed. But he believes it, or if you please, judges that it was so; I do not. The uniting of ideas produces a conception, common both to him who believes and to him who does not (p. 97).

Moreover, there are judgements which contain only a single idea, *e.g.*, "God exists" (footnote, p. 98). Here the only idea concerned is that of God. This judgement then cannot consist of a union of different ideas. But you may say that this judgement consists in uniting the idea of existence to that of God. That would be an error; existence is not a distinct idea, which we can unite with or separate from any other idea at our pleasure. Whether we form the idea of a mermaid or of God, we form the idea of something, of a *being* with certain attributes; if we seek to enlarge our conception by adding the idea of existence, we achieve nothing; the idea remains just what it was before; it was always the idea of a *being* of a certain sort.

The passage from mere conception to belief cannot therefore consist, as some have supposed, in the addition of the idea of existence to the idea we had already formed; for, first, the idea already formed was, as we have said the idea of a being, and secondly, if we did add another idea to the idea already formed, we should be *altering* our conception, and what we now believe would be something different from what we previously conceived. But *ex hypothesi*, that is not the case; what we are considering is the difference between conceiving something and believing that same thing, or more accurately between entertaining a proposition and believing that same proposition (pp. 96-97).

Hume concludes that since the difference between mere conception and belief does not consist in a difference in what is conceived, it must consist in a difference in our manner of conceiving of it (p. 96).

There can I think be no doubt that Hume had his eye on the famous Ontological Proof of the existence of God[1] in this passage. That is why he takes the proposition that God exists as his instance on p. 96.

His contention that the idea of existence is not a distinct idea different from the idea of any object, is an anticipation of Kant's statement that "existence is not a predicate", on which his refutation of the ontological argument is founded. Hume's observations, brief and allusive as they are, seem to me to

---

[1]This proof runs as follows: God is by definition perfect ; non-existence is an imperfection. Therefore God exists.

explain more clearly than Kant does, just why "existence is not a predicate".

He puts the matter most succinctly in Treatise Book I, Part II, Sect. VI. "To reflect on anything simply, and to reflect on it as existent, are nothing different from each other. . . . Whatever we conceive, we conceive to be existent. Any idea we please to form is the idea of a being; and the idea of a being is any idea we please to form". It is, therefore, logically necessary, when we conceive of *anything*, to conceive it as existing. But this is just what the defenders of the ontological argument said was a *peculiarity* of the conception of God. "I cannot conceive God unless as existing", says Descartes.

To put it another way, it is indeed inconceivable that there should be a God who does not exist, just as it is inconceivable that there should be a table or a mermaid which does not exist. But that does not imply that it is inconceivable that there should be no God.

Why does Hume not explicitly mention the ontological argument, either in the section on the idea of existence, or in the section on belief? I can only suggest, first, that he regarded it as merely one of the many misguided attempts of philosophers to demonstrate matters of fact, the impossibility of which he claims to show in general where he treats of knowledge and probability, and secondly, that he prefers to leave the ontologists to infer from his words the nature of the special fallacy they have committed, by way of an ironical tribute to the intelligence which he conceives, but does not believe, them to possess.

Let us return to Hume's account of belief.

The difference between mere conception and belief lies not in any difference in the ideas conceived but in the manner in which we conceive them. Provided we interpret the phrase "manner in which we conceive them" and the word "idea" in the widest possible way, and do not follow Hume in his attempt to specify this manner further, we can scarcely but agree with him so far. Nor could it easily be denied that this manner is something that can be "felt", an impression of reflection.

It is Hume's further specification of the manner of conception that has aroused criticism. Belief, he says, consists in the "vivacity" of the idea conceived. Looking at the question from his own psychological point of view (p. 98) he can come to no other conclusion. An idea is for him an image; "Our ideas are copied from our impressions"; what an idea represents is the combination of impressions which it resembles. The difference between an idea conceived and an idea believed must not alter what is represented by the idea. The only conceivable intrinsic difference that will not alter it is a difference in what he calls "vivacity"; just as the only difference you can make in a shade of colour, without altering its hue, is to make it brighter or less bright.

This analogy of the shade of colour is, I think, unfortunate. It suggests that what he means by the vivacity of an idea believed is brightness of colour and distinctness of outline. This is not quite consistent with what he says on the next page, where he tries, by means of a variety of synonymous terms, to make clearer what he means. The idea believed, he there says, *feels* different from the mere conception, and this difference of feeling he calls "its superior *force*, or *vivacity*, or *solidity*, or *firmness*, or *steadiness*". He also seeks to identify the quality he refers to by its effects; it is what makes "realities more present to us then fictions, causes them to weigh more in our thought, and gives them a superior influence on the passions and imagination".

All this suggests something other than mere brightness of a picture. The term "force" already suggests power to influence the workings of our mind in the ways he afterwards mentions; "firmness" and "steadiness" suggests rather fixity, freedom from variation, than brightness and distinctness of outline. In the end he is content to say that it is something familiar, whose "true and proper name is *belief*, which is a term that everybody sufficiently understands in common life", something for which there is no other precise term.

Two more points must be noted to complete our account of Hume's description of the peculiar quality of the believed idea.

First, though a feeling, it is not a feeling distinct from the idea but accompanying it as desire accompanies the idea of something pleasant.

Second, the feeling though familiar and lacking any other name, is not quite unique. Both these points are made in the Appendix to the Treatise.

With regard to the first, he says that no such distinct impression is discoverable to introspection; that there is no need to assume it in order to explain what we do find in introspection, *i.e.*, firmness and steadiness; and that if there were such a thing its causes would be inexplicable.

With regard to the second, he says that if it were unique, we must despair of explaining its causes by analogy with any other phenomenon of the human mind. Fortunately, he finds that it is the same quality, in a rather lower degree, as that which characterises an impression and constitutes our assent to its reality; he is thus able to explain how ideas become enlivened; the impressions with which they are associated impart to them a share of their vivacity.

Let us now turn to the criticisms usually brought against Hume's contention.

These may be summed up as follows: If belief consists in a feeling of vivacity, then differences in strength of belief should consist in differences of strength of this feeling. But (1) we seem to have little or no strength of feeling about some of the propositions of whose truth we are most firmly persuaded, and (2) we often conceive in the liveliest possible manner situations in whose reality we do not believe.

As instances of (1) propositions such as $2+2=4$, which Hume would call "relations of ideas", are often taken. With regard to such propositions Hume forestalls the criticism on p. 97, though perhaps he does not express his view in the best possible way. He says that it is easy to discover what is the difference between believing and disbelieving a proposition, in the case of "propositions that are proved by intuition or demonstration". "In that case the person who assents not only conceives the ideas according to the proposition,[1] but is necessarily determined to conceive them in that particular manner"; because, in short, the contradictory of the proposition is inconceivable, being a self-contradiction. The trouble arises in the case of factual propositions, where both the proposition and its contradictory are not only conceivable but conceived; what then is the difference between the proposition which we believe and its opposite which we do not?

[1] By proposition Hume here means "sentence".

Now we can either interpret Hume as meaning that when we say we believe a demonstrable proposition, we mean something different by "belief" from that which we mean when we say that we believe a factual proposition; in the first case we mean "necessarily determined" conception, in the second case vivacious conception; or we can interpret Hume as meaning that our assent to a demonstrable proposition is not a case of belief but of knowledge. This would be in keeping with his account of knowledge in Part III, Section I of the Treatise. In either case the objection is forestalled. The kind of belief he defines as "vivacity" is the assurance we repose in a factual proposition after considering both it and its contradictory. His definition is not meant to cover assent to propositions expressing relations of ideas, such as $2+2=4$.

But what if the objector cites some very well-established empirical belief, such as that the earth goes round the sun ? Here surely is a case where the opposite of the proposition is conceivable, but where the strength of our belief is altogether out of proportion to the strength of any feelings that attach themselves to the proposition believed. On the contrary, it is just *because* we are so firmly persuaded of the truth of the proposition, because we regard the question as so definitely settled, that we have no strong feelings about it. We do not, as has been pointed out, "sweat with conviction" on such matters.

In reply to this objection I would draw a distinction; a "well-established" empirical belief may mean one for which there is in my experience very good evidence, including testimony perhaps, or it may mean one which has been long and firmly established in my mind. A belief may be very firmly established in my mind, even if I have none or little evidence to support it; *i.e.*, it may be an inveterate prejudice; similarly, a proposition may have long been well-supported by my experience without having ever been entertained or assented to by me before. Or, of course, a belief may be well-established in both senses.

Now, when I first entertain and assent to a proposition for which my experience provides very strong evidence—for instance, when in a book by some gifted observer of human nature I read a brilliant generalisation, new to me, but exactly tallying with my own experience—then the manner in which I conceive this proposition is surely just what Hume describes. The evidence of my experience lends strength to my belief, it enlivens, enforces, bestows a certain feeling upon the idea; this feeling, it is not unplausible to say, *is* my emphatic assent to the proposition. And it is the difference between assenting to a proposition and just entertaining it which Hume is attempting to describe.

But as time goes on the generalisation becomes familiar; I become accustomed to assenting to the proposition, and to acting in the light of it, every time circumstances suggest it. It ceases to be new and exciting ; and all violence and vigour of assent are lost to it. In what now does the "strength of my belief" consist? It consists plainly in the strength, *i.e.*, the regularity of operation, of a habit. Though my assent may now be quite languid, you can be pretty sure I shall not deny the proposition, except in order to deceive or provoke, and that I shall not act in any manner that would not serve my purposes if it were true. Moreover, my assent, though languid, will come with that felt familiar facility, that smooth click, which only habit gives.

Now I cannot honestly say for Hume that he clearly recognised that what is most often meant by a belief is not a particular act of assent, but a disposition or habit of mind. But it is noteworthy that the predicates firmness and steadiness, by which he characterises an idea assented to, are more naturally applicable to a habit than an individual representation.

We can now sum up Hume's account of assent, in order better to meet the second barrel of the stock objection, viz., that we often conceive an idea very vivaciously without believing it. According to Hume, whether we assent to an analytic proposition as a matter of knowledge, or whether we assent to a synthetic proposition as a matter of belief, the idea must be steadied and fixed to the exclusion of incompatible alternatives. In the case of an analytic proposition this is ensured by the inconceivability of all incompatible alternatives. In the case of a synthetic proposition it is effected by the regularity of past experience. The idea believed represents what has always happened in situations like the present one. All incompatible ideas represent what has only sometimes or never happened in such situations; there is nothing to fix them in the mind to the exclusion of rival ideas.

The emphasis in this account is on the steadiness rather than the vividness of the idea believed. Those who urge the objection that we often conceive an idea very vivaciously without believing it miss this point. Hume's answer to them is that the sort of ideas they mean are vivified indeed by some associated impression, but, not being steadied in the way we have described, are not genuine beliefs.

Hume discusses these pseudo-beliefs at length in Sect. IX "Of the effects of other relations and other habits". We must now consider what he says of them.

2. *States of mind which simulate belief* (Treatise Book I, Part III, Sect. IX)

Hume, as we have seen, admits three relations which originally associate ideas in the imagination; resemblance, contiguity and causation. Any idea evoked by a present impression with which it is associated in any of these ways is enlivened by the association. This he asserts to be an empirical fact. Belief is defined as a lively idea associated with a present impression. Presumably, therefore, any association with a present impression converts an idea into a belief. Far from it; it is a fundamental tenet of Hume's that only the causal relationship gives rise to genuine belief.

Hume now faces this difficulty. His answer is, in effect, to distinguish two things. During the course of a day, many ideas will be suggested to me in a great variety of ways; pictures will suggest the ideas of scenes and persons resembling them, hills will suggest the ideas of vales that lie beyond them; the statements of my fellow men will suggest to me all manner of ideas. Many of these ideas will become enlivened by their association with present impressions and command my fleeting and momentary assent. This is one class of ideas. But besides this I have another system of ideas, which, by their settled order and their regular connexion with the impressions of sense and memory, command my habitual assent, and which I dignify by the term "realities".

These latter ideas, for instance, to take Hume's example, his idea of Rome, are not particular psychological occurrences, each with a date. They are classes of such occurrences, whose members occur according to the settled habits of the mind and are enlivened by customary connexion with impressions of memory. It was a relatively permanent fact about Mr. Hume that he was disposed to assent to certain conceptions of the history and geography of Rome. "All this", he says, "and everything else which I believe are nothing but ideas, though by their force and settled order, arising from custom and the relation of cause and effect, they distinguish themselves from the other ideas, which are merely the offspring of the imagination".

I would like to suggest as precisely as I can what I think Hume means in the foregoing somewhat loosely worded passage.

The ideas called realities are marked by "force and settled order". This means that they are assented to with some promptness and vigour ("force") as a matter of habit ("settled") provided they occur in a certain pattern of spatio-temporal relations ("order"); e.g., I habitually assent to a certain representation of the city of Rome, which represents it on the banks of the Tiber and south of the Alps. A similar representation of the city, which, however, placed it north of the Alps, would not command my assent in the same way. Such beliefs then are habitual beliefs, habits of assent, even if they are (as in this case) particular as opposed to general beliefs.

But such habitual particular beliefs can only arise as the result of habits of a more general kind. It is because experience has accustomed me to trust in the statements of historians, the fidelity of copyists, the reliability of cartographers, etc., that I form this particular belief. These general habits can only be produced by regular conjunctions in experience (Hume here maintains), and only the general habits can generate the particular habits of assent which are particular beliefs, whose objects we call realities, such as the city of Rome. This is what is meant by "the force and settled order arising from custom and the relation of cause and effect".

This view is not incompatible with the view that genuine belief has a special feel about. If genuine beliefs are habits of assent, each act of assent in accordance with such a habit will have about it the peculiar smooth facility which characterises all habitual acts. It becomes increasingly clear as Hume's argument goes on that it is the "firmness" and "steadiness", characteristic of habitual assent, rather than the brightness of the image or the degree of felt conviction, which is the essential characteristic of a genuine belief, and which only constant conjunction in experience can produce.

Turning to the relations of resemblance and contiguity, he points out that these may operate in two ways.

First, an impression, for instance the sight of a portrait of my friend, or of the last milestone on the road home, may evoke and enliven the ideas of my friend, or of my home. In these cases the relationship does heighten my belief by adding to the vivacity of the idea; but my friend, the subject of the picture, and my home situated near the milestone, are in these cases items in my system of realities; they are already believed in on other grounds, of memory and inference. As Hume points out, unless I already believed that the picture was a portrait of my friend, it would not enliven my idea of him at all.

Secondly, a picture may suggest a quite new idea of something like it, or the place where my friend used to live may suggest the idea of him coming round the next corner to meet me. We may give a momentary assent to these suggestions; but we cannot incorporate them in our system of habitual beliefs; they lack the necessary credentials. For the same impression may by the same relation evoke another and incompatible suggestion at any moment. The picture suggests the idea of an historical event one moment, of an event on the stage the next. The place suggests my friend doing one thing one moment, something different the next. "The mind foresees and anticipates the change; and even from the first instant *feels* the looseness of its actions, and the weak hold it has of its object".

These other relations can then, by themselves, only produce a sort of flickering shortlived vivification of an idea, quite different from the steadiness and firmness which mark an idea associated by custom with a present impression. When added to the relation of cause and effect they reinforce belief, as Hume shows by various examples. But they cannot by themselves produce it; for they cannot give to the idea that firmness and steadiness which only custom can give.

This then, as we have already seen, is Hume's answer to the second barrel of the stock objection. Ideas may, indeed, be in a way enlivened by a great variety of psychological processes. But none of these, except constant conjunction in experience of similar impressions, gives to the idea enlivened the feeling of firmness, of enjoying a connexion with the enlivening impression denied to other and incompatible ideas. This lack of firmness prevents such quasi-beliefs from having, at least in normal minds, the same influence on our passions and our actions.

This feeling of firmness and steadiness, the opposite of "looseness", is, I think, according to Hume, the very same with that felt "determination of the mind" which is the impression from which the idea of necessary connexion is derived. And it is nothing but the consciousness of custom at work. Habitual actions, whether mental or physical, have a firm inevitable feel about them; we feel tied to them as we do them. The existence of habit, both in operation and in readiness is, according to Hume, felt. (Compare Treatise, Book I, Part I, Sect. VII, p. 28).

But there is another difficulty which Hume foresees. A belief, he says, is an idea enlivened by association with a present impression, and steadied by the operation of a custom founded on constant conjunction. But why must it be constant conjunction of past *impressions*? Is it true that only the causal relation, only constant conjunctions in *experience* can produce belief? No; Hume sees that something else both should in theory be able to produce it, and in fact does; education. We believe what we have repeatedly been told. Settled and determinate habits of association can be produced by constant conjunctions between the *ideas* suggested by the discourse of others, just as well as by constant conjunctions between *impressions* in experience.

Of ordinary people Hume thinks it is true that more than half their beliefs are produced by education. Philosophers, however, he says, do not "recognise" education (p. 118). Beliefs resulting purely from education, unsupported by experience corroborating either the propositions believed or the reliability of the educators, are not epistemologically respectable.

The reasons Hume gives to explain why philosophers do not "recognise" education are (a) that "Education is an artificial and not a natural cause", and (b) that "its maxims are frequently contrary to reason and even to themselves in different times and places". By reason (a) he means that the associations of ideas derived from education depend on the wishes and motives of educators, and human wishes have no necessary connexion with what actually occurs. By reason (b) he means that the maxims of educators are frequently self-contradictory, and frequently contrary to "reason" in the sense of being either logically absurd, or contrary to experience.

It is easy to see how reflection on the arbitrary nature and self-contradictoriness of educators' maxims would give rise to just that feeling of "looseness" and unsteadiness which Hume says is the opposite of belief. But the observation that educators' maxims are frequently contradicted by experience raises the difficult question why we prefer experience, which, after all, frequently suggests mutually contradictory conclusions, to the authority of educators, prophets, astrologers and the like. This question will be considered later. (Ch. VI, 3.)

It is time to give a final estimate of Hume's account of belief. It has, I think, two faults.

The first is that Hume appears to think that he is trying to describe a *single* thing; a certain single, simple feeling which believed ideas have, of which such terms as "force", "vivacity", "steadiness", "firmness", etc., are alternative descriptions. I would suggest that what he is trying to describe is really a class of complex states of affairs. It is a mark of belief that the idea believed is vividly imagined and holds our involuntary attention, it is a mark of belief that the idea believed is steady and habitual; it is a mark of belief that the steady conception of the idea comes with the click of custom in suitable conditions; it is a mark of belief that we feel and act as would be appropriate if the idea were true. Hume describes these marks very well. But no one of them (except possibly the last, since it may be held to include all the others) is by itself a necessary or sufficient criterion of genuine belief; rather a sufficient number of the marks must be present in a sufficient degree.

Much the same problem would arise if we tried to define "health". That the bodily organs are in a normal physiological condition, that the person "feels well", that he can and does perform normal activities successfully, all these are marks of health. No one of them *is* health, nor is health a mysterious something distinct from the marks of it.

Hume's contention with regard to cause and effect amounts to this, that only constant conjunctions in experience can produce certain of the marks of belief, steadiness, consistency, habit-feeling, etc., without a certain degree of at least some of which there is no belief.

The second fault is that Hume seems to attach too much weight to the association of the idea believed with a present impression of the senses or of memory. My belief that there is bacon and eggs for breakfast because I smell them may, indeed, be plausibly defined as a lively idea associated with a present impression. But my belief that silver is more fusible than lead, or that if Hitler had invaded England in 1940 he would have conquered it, may well rest on past impressions which I do not now actually recall. I may even be unable to recall the evidence on which a belief rests; but that does not make me abandon it.

This fault is not very important, as Hume's main position stands, provided it is true that the idea believed is always associated in the ways he describes with some impressions, whether past or present, remembered or forgotten.

F

CHAPTER VI

PROBABILITY[1]

1. *The probability of chances and the probability of causes*
   (Treatise Book I, Part III, Sects. XI and XII)

HUME distinguishes two main senses in which a proposition
may be called probable.

(1) The sense in which he used the word "probability" as
opposed to "knowledge" at the beginning of Part III of the
Treatise, following Locke. In this sense it is probable that the
rays of light passed through a convex lens will converge; they
always have hitherto. We merely refuse to call it a certainty
because no logical demonstration is possible; the supposition
that they will diverge is not self-contradictory. This is definitely
a philosopher's use of the term. "Probable" reasoning, by this
way of speaking, is all reasoning that depends on "the presumption that the unobserved will resemble the observed".
It is opposed to demonstrative reasoning which rests on the
principle that a proposition whose contradictory is self-
contradictory is true.

(2) The sense in which we should say that it is probable
that I shall recover from influenza, or that I shall not draw
a Queen from a complete pack of cards, turned face downwards,
at the first attempt. In this sense "probability" is still opposed
to "certainty"; but we deny certainty for a different sort of
reason; our reason is not the absence of demonstration, but the
presence of some grounds for expecting the proposition to
prove false, grounds of the same kind as those which lead us to
expect it to be true, but less weighty. Most people similar to

---

[1]For a more detailed exposition of the kind of view of probability recommended in this chapter, and for a defence of it against certain abstruse
mathematical objections, the reader is referred to "Mind", July, 1940,
art. "On probability" by G. H. von Wright.

me have recovered from influenza, a few have died. I am going to pick one of the cards on the table; 48 of those cards are not Queens; but 4 are.

Now these two cases, the influenza and the cards, differ in kind; the first Hume would call a case of the probability of causes, the second a case of the probability of chances.

We may put the difference in this way. In both cases probable reasoning in sense (1), *i.e.*, inference from past observations, plays a part. But it plays a different part in each. In the case of the influenza, past observation gives the proportion of recoveries to deaths, say, 50 to 1, which I somehow transfer to the present instance, and say the probability of my recovery is 50 to 1. In the second case, past observations give me the assurance that the cards do not change the devices on their faces while laid on the table, or, if I have not inspected the pack, that packs of playing cards normally contain only four Queens, and that the person who assures me that this is a normal pack usually tells the truth. The proportion of 48 to 4 which determines the numerical probability of the proposition is not a proportion of past observations; it is a proportion of present existences, either inferred from past observations or known from present observations.

The difference can also be seen by reflecting that in the former case, if all past influenza patients had recovered, it would still be logically possible that I should die; but if there were no Queens in the pack it would be logically impossible that I should pick one out.

Hume considers *the probability of chances* first, because he thinks that its nature throws light on the probability of causes, which is a more important question, and plainly more germane to the general issue he is dealing with. What he says about it contains two elements, an epistemological, and a psychological. His epistemological contentions concerning the probability of chances, are, as far as they go, in my opinion, true. His psychological contentions are more dubious, and contain difficulties for his general theory.

His epistemological contentions are as follows:

(1) By chance is meant the negation of a cause. Chance, he also says, is nothing real. Therefore, by the former statement, he does not mean that there really are uncaused events; but

that when a persons says "it is a matter of chance whether the die falls on this side or one of the other sides", he means "no ascertainable causes determine which side it shall fall on". There are, of course, Hume thinks, concealed causes at work, though the vulgar do not always suspect it; they think "chances" and "luck" are real things in the world.

(2) Since a chance is a mere absence of a known cause, all chances are "equal". No one chance can of itself be "better" than another. If there is no ascertainable cause at work to make the die fall on side x rather than side y, the chances are equal. The chance of x can only of itself be superior to the chance of y, if the past behaviour of the die, or similar objects, suggests that it more often falls that way up; but in that case we have evidence of a cause at work, and the superior probability is a case of the probability of causes.

(3) A chance can only be more probable as a chance, if it is really a number of chances combined together. One composite chance is superior to another composite chance if it is composed of a greater number of simple chances.

(4) The relative magnitudes of composite chances can only be calculated within a given "family" of chances of a finite number. For instance, it must first be established that the die has six sides, that four of the sides are marked with a cross and two with a circle, that it will lie on one of them, that their number and marking will not be altered in the fall, etc. We can then say that it is 2 to 1 on a cross coming uppermost.

Having established these propositions (Treatise pp. 127-8), Hume then asks why we are more inclined to believe that· a cross will come uppermost than that a circle will.

He points out that no "comparison of mere ideas", *i.e.*, no demonstrative argument, can lead us to this conclusion. There is no logical necessity that the event should fall on that side where there is a superior number of chances; on the contrary we know a circle may perfectly well turn up.

But is it perhaps a logical necessity that in the circumstances described it is more *likely* or *probable* that a cross will turn up? We feel it is; but what do we mean here by *likelihood*? There is nothing we can mean except that the number of chances of a cross is greater than the number of chances of a circle. But this is not a deduction from the given facts about the die, its number of sides and its marking. It is simply a general way of describing them. In this sense of likelihood, it is a mere tautology to say that if there are six sides, four marked with a cross and two with a circle, and the die will fall on one of them, then the number of chances of a cross is greater than the number of chances of a circle, and that if this is so, then a cross is more likely that a circle. These are all simply different ways of describing the data. The question is how these data influence our expectations. Not, so far as Hume can see, by means of any chain of reasoning; therefore, he presumes, by a psychological process. And he then proceeds to describe what he thinks this psychological process is, with all the loving care of a philosopher for one of his pet theoretical offspring.

The question is how the idea (*i.e.*, image) of a side marked with a cross acquires greater force and vivacity than that of a side marked with a circle. And he has no difficulty in answering this question. The image of the side with a cross is really a fusion of four separate and similar images, each with an equal amount of vivacity of its own, and its vivacity is the sum of the vivacities of those four images; the image of the side with a circle is a fusion of only two similar images, each with the same amount of vivacity. The more vivacious fused image overpowers, but does not destroy the less vivacious fused image; this state of double expectation, expecting two events, but one more strongly than the other, is probable expectation.

It is at this point that I begin to suspect that I see why Hume took as his instance a die such as he described, rather than one of the normal type, with sides marked from 1 to 6. The normal die could not generate this simple psychological process of image-fusion. The four images of the sides marked respectively with 1, 2, 3 and 4 dots could not fuse into a single image. I shall consider later, in connexion with the probability of causes, what Hume should have said in order to avoid this difficulty.

Having followed Hume into his dubious psychological explanation, let us consider this conundrum further from an epistemological point of view, and see if we can suggest some more *reassuring* account of this species of reasoning.

How does the knowledge that the die has six sides, four marked with a cross, two with a circle, and that it will lie with one of them turned upwards, make it reasonable to expect a cross rather than a circle? A possibility suggests itself which Hume does not explore. The inference may be a case of empirical reasoning from past experience; dice similar to this one have always tended, in any considerable number of throws, to fall an equal number of times on each of the sides; therefore a die marked like this one tends to fall twice as often with a cross uppermost as with a circle. And what has more often happened in the past is more likely to happen in the future. That is, the probability of chances reduces itself to a special case of the probability of causes.

This suggestion, however, will not do as it stands, for the following reason. The conclusion justified by the alleged evidence is that in any considerable number of throws the crosses will turn up about twice as often as the circles. What we want is a conclusion about this particular throw. And the only way we can get it from this evidence is as follows. The throw in question will be one of a number of throws; of this number about twice as many will be crosses as will be circles; therefore this throw has twice as many chances of being one of the throws that give a cross as it has of being one of the throws that give a circle, since there will be twice as many of them. The probability of causes therefore only yields a conclusion *about a particular event* by the aid of the probability of chances.

The conclusion suggested is that the calculation of chances is an antonomous species of reasoning whose validity we accept on its own merits, and which is used whenever we make a probable inference about a particular event on the evidence of either statistical frequencies or "mathematical odds". This conclusion is accepted by many philosophers.

But the validity of this species of reasoning is mysterious. It is not demonstration and it is not induction; it seems to be even more mysterious than induction. Hume says it is just something we in fact do, of which he can give a psychological explanation. Can we do better than this? Can we give any kind of recommendation of it?

Let us return to the die. We may accept three propositions:

(1) The equality of the chances together with the respective

numbers of the circles and crosses is the ground of the probable expectation of a cross.

(2) The behaviour of the die in the past, or of similar objects, is the ultimate evidence for the equality of the chances. For any tendency of one side to turn up more often than another, or any corresponding inequality in the behaviour of any comparable object, would be taken as evidence that some cause was present more often than not which made it fall on one side rather than on any other, and therefore that the chances were not equal ; this would still be the case however much was known about the shape and composition of the die.

(3) From these two propositions it follows that the equality in the past behaviour of the die, or of comparable objects, together with the present observed facts about the number and marking of the sides, is the ultimate evidence on which the probable expectation of a cross for any particular throw is founded.

Now if it can be shown that the probable expectation follows directly from this evidence by any intelligible process of reasoning, our problem will be solved. The intermediate proposition about the numbers of equal chances will be by-passed, and can be regarded as a mere convenient summary of the real evidence, a summary which is nevertheless philosophically misleading.

Now from the equality of the past behaviour of the die it can be inferred by induction, on the principle that the unobserved will resemble the observed, that in any considerable number of throws, each side will turn up about the same number of times.[1] From this it follows by logical entailment, since four of the sides bear a cross and two a circle, that crosses will turn up about twice as often as circles. From this it follows logically that if I always, as a matter of habit, predict a cross, I shall be right twice as often as I am wrong. And from this it follows logically that on each occasion on which I predict a cross I am predicting in accordance with a method which succeeds twice as often as it fails.

Now it does seem plausible to say that to predict in accordance with a method which succeeds more often than it fails is *reasonable*, in the ordinary sense of the word.

---

[1] It is unfortunately extremely difficult to formulate this statement more precisely.

Turning to the *probability of causes*, we again find an epistemological and a psychological element in Hume's contentions.

The epistemological contentions consist in a description of the more external conditions under which probability judgements are made; or, if you prefer it, under which sentences of the form "E is probable" are properly uttered in the ordinary use of language.

The psychological contentions consist in a description of the inner psychological mechanisms connecting the outer conditions with the utterance of the probability statement.

On the epistemological side, two types of probability judgement are distinguished, the unreflective and the reflective.

Unreflective judgements of probability are made, according to Hume, under two types of conditions (pp. 133–134); (a) when the event called probable is like only a few past events which have happened in circumstances similar to the present situation ; *i.e.*, when we judge on the evidence of a few past cases only, not enough to give certainty ; (b) when there is not merely paucity but contrariety in our experience, and the event called probable is like what happened in many similar situations in the past, but unlike what happened in some.

This account seems to me true, provided we remember that sometimes special psychological factors, permanent or temporary, make people judge with certainty even under these conditions..

Hume thinks that the reflective type of probability judgement is far more common in our reasoning (p. 134). In this type we recall and count up the relevant past cases known either by memory or previous inference. We then assign to the event a numerical probability value equal to the fraction obtained by dividing the number of comparable cases in which a similar event occurred by the total number of comparable cases.

This is evidently a rudimentary description of what we call "statistical method". And it is a very inadequate account. Experience of cyclical, progressive and irregular fluctuations in the frequency of many conjunctions quickly leads us to distrust it. What we look for in statistical evidence is either a proportion which is approximately constant in any random selection of cases, or, failing that, a description of the fluctuations either in terms of periodic cycles or of special factors on which they depend. We are never content with a mere overall proportion.

Hume points out that both reflective and unreflective judgements of probability, as opposed to certainty, are also made when the resemblance between the present case and the past cases is imperfect. This species of reasoning is called reasoning by analogy (p. 142).

On the psychological side Hume accounts for the hesitation characterising unreflective probability judgements by the weakness of the habit set up where there are only a few similar cases in the past, and by the opposition of contrary habits where there is a contrariety in our experience. To this account we may provisionally assent, and pass to the difficult question of the reflective probability judgement.

In the reflective probability judgement we actually recall the past cases and count them up. In the past, 19 ships have returned safely for every one that was wrecked (p. 135). I now consider the chances of a particular ship which is putting to sea. According to Hume the 19 images of ships returning safely into harbour blend and form a single image, which is 19 times as forcible and vivacious as the single image of a shipwreck.

This is plainly nonsense. The fused image resulting from the blending of images of full-rigged ships, barques, barquentines, brigs, schooners and luggers, differing in almost every respect of hull-form, and arrangement of spars and sails, is just the sort of image which Berkeley and Hume maintained, in criticism of Locke's Theory of Abstract Ideas, to be impossible. And even if such "generic" images do occur, as some modern psychologists assert, they are not what is wanted in this sort of thinking. What is wanted is a lively image of this particular ship, say a top-sail schooner, returning safely to her own particular home port.

It is important to see clearly the difficulty which Hume sought to dispose of by this expedient. Hitherto, he has always represented factual inferences, whether certain or probable, as

due to the operation of custom. But, as he observes in this
section of the Treatise (p. 134), in considering the unreflective
probability judgement, "When we follow only the habitual
determination of the mind, we make the transition without
any reflection. . . . As the custom depends not on any
deliberation, it operates immediately, without allowing any
time for reflection". The force of custom then is fully spent in
the unreflective judgement. It is the past experiences, not the
conscious recollection of them, which cause the habitual
transition.

How then, when we do reflect, do the recollections of the
past cases influence belief? Not, it is evident, by custom;
therefore, in some other way. Here is a new cause of belief, or
at least a new causal factor that modifies the degree of belief;
and it seems to Hume to be present both in the probability of
chances and the probability of causes. In the case of the die
we have a number of particular ideas, some of them
representing a cross turning up, some a circle; in the case of
the ships we have a number of ideas, some representing ships
returning safely, some representing them being wrecked. In
both cases it is the superior number of one kind of idea over
the other that determines our belief.

In the Enquiry (Sect. VI, para. 46), the fusion of images is
dropped. There he says:

"But finding a greater number of sides (of the die) concur
in one event than in the other, the mind is carried more
frequently to that event, and meets it oftener in revolving
the various possibilities or chances, on which the ultimate
result depends. This concurrence of several views in one
particular event begets immediately, by an inexplicable
contrivance of nature, the sentiment of belief".

This passage from the Enquiry suggests an alternative
account, more in keeping with Hume's theory of general ideas.

According to that theory (Treatise Book I, Part I, Sect. VII),
the various particular images of different ships returning safe
to port, associated with one another by resemblance and with
the expression "ship returning safe to port" by customary
conjunction, are all actualisations of the general idea of a ship
returning safe to port. The general idea consists in a disposition
of the mind to run through such images in association with the

verbal expression. The "vivacity" therefore of a general idea will consist in the vivacity of the particular ideas in which it is actualised; and these will be more vivacious if they are ideas of memory, not merely of imagination.

Hume could, therefore, plausibly have said that the idea of this particular ship returning is enlivened by the vivacity of the general idea of which it is an actualisation, that idea being lively on account of the number of memory ideas which it can claim among its actualisations, and which in a reflective probability judgement have been counted up.

2. *Habit and expectation*

Hume has also a more fundamental psychological question to raise. Both in the reflective and unreflective probability judgement we judge in accordance with the presumption that the future will resemble the past, the unobserved the observed (pp. 134-5, see also Part III, Sect. VI, p. 92). How this happens has not yet been fully explained.

What we have been told is that the present impression, *e.g.* flame, being associated by resemblance with past similar impressions, and they by contiguity with what followed them, *i.e.* heat, evokes and enlivens the ideas of what has followed on similar impressions in the past, and that when this happens frequently the transition becomes habitual. But we have not been told why the lively idea of heat so evoked is taken not merely as a compelling picture of what *has* happened, but as a compelling picture of what is now *about* to happen. How does it come to fit itself on to the present impression as a picture of what will *follow* it? Why do we inevitably tend to form a picture of future developments, and to model that picture on the past?

Hume asserts roundly that the principle that the future will resemble the past "is not founded on arguments of any kind" (p. 135). It is, he says "derived from habit, by which we are determined to expect for the future the same train of objects to which we have been accustomed". We are told no more.

We must note that the repetition of impressions cannot by itself set up a habit of expectation. Habit, according to Hume, consists in doing something, simply because we have done *that same thing* before (Treatise Book I, Part III, Sect. VIII, p. 105; Enquiry, Sect. V, Part I, para. 36). It cannot, therefore, account for our *expecting* something, because we have often *experienced* it before, or because we have often *remembered* it before.

We are, therefore, driven to conclude that Hume regarded the forming of expectations on the model of the past as an original inborn habit, *i.e.* an instinct. Only if we presuppose this original habit can we see how "when we have lived any time, and have been accustomed to the uniformity of nature, we acquire a general habit, by which we always transfer the known to the unknown, and conceive the latter to resemble the former" (Enquiry, Sect. IX, para. 84, footnote).

Hume could have given a more plausible account of this instinct if he had considered thinking in closer relation with action.

What makes us consider the future, it might be said, is that we have desires to be satisfied. In satisfying our desires we have, along with all other living things, a tendency to repeat those actions which have been successful in the past; we do it with confidence when they have always and often been successful; with less confidence, when they have only been tried out on a few occasions; with hesitation when they have sometimes proved unsuccessful. In repeating these actions we use our memory images of the past cases, with all their attendants and consequences, as guiding pictures; so used, and perhaps modified, as the action is, to fit in with the peculiarities of the present situation, they come to be regarded as representations of the future.

As our actions become more complex, and the satisfactions to which they tend more distant, the guiding pictures become more and more important, and the formation of them becomes itself an activity useful to the satisfaction of desires. Ways of forming them that prove unsuccessful are dropped in favour of ways of forming them that are successful; and ways of forming them which give shifting and inconsistent pictures, useless for guiding our long-term activities, are dropped for that reason. This is Hume's use of general rules founded on our experience of the understanding and its operations (p. 148). A few examples may make my meaning clearer. The boxer who has repeatedly stopped his opponent's rushes with a straight left, repeats the action. This simple action to satisfy an

immediate need requires little or no guiding imagery. The
billiards or croquet player who plans a series of consecutive
strokes on the model of his past successes will have much
more need of guiding pictures. The General who plans a
campaign in accordance with the lessons of military history will
need guiding pictures so complex that he must call in the aid
of maps, figures, tables, graphs and charts to assist his
imagination, and must make sure that they are compiled by the
most reliable methods.

The biological hypothesis that an organism tends to repeat
the behaviour which has brought it satisfaction in the past, on
which this account is based, was probably little known, or
unknown, in Hume's day; but I think he might well have
accepted the account as in keeping with his general line of
thought. I do not propose, in what follows, to attempt to
reformulate all Hume's contentions in the light of this
hypothesis. The reader may attempt to do it for himself if he
pleases.

3. *"Unphilosophical probability"* (Treatise Book I, Part III,
   Sects. IX, XIII, XV, and Part IV, Sect. I)

Let us first sum up Hume's account of probability as we
have so far considered it.

Subjectively considered, probability, or rational belief, is
an idea enlivened by a present impression and steadied and
fortified against rival ideas by its being conceived in accordance
with a habit, and in some cases by the fusion of ideas of similar
cases. Objectively considered, the probability of an idea
consists in the resemblance between it, taken together with the
impression that evokes it, and events that have repeatedly
occurred in the past. Subjectively considered, its essence is the
smooth click of custom and fusion of images, objectively
considered its essence is repeated occurrence of similar
conjunctions of events. The latter is the cause of the former.

Forming probable beliefs in this way is something we do
by nature; and no amount of sceptical arguments will stop us.

> "Nature, by an absolute and uncontrollable necessity, has
> determined us to judge as well as to breathe and feel;
> nor can we any more forbear viewing certain objects in
> a stronger and fuller light, upon account of their

customary connexion with a present impression, than we can hinder ourselves from thinking, as long as we are awake, or seeing the surrounding bodies, when we turn our eyes towards them in bright sunshine". (Treatise Book I, Part IV, Sect. I, p. 179.)

This is, however, not the only way in which we form lively ideas. As we have seen, ideas are also enlivened by relations with present impressions other than that of cause and effect, to wit resemblance and contiguity; and they are steadied and fixed by habits based not on repetitions of similar impressions, but on repetitions of similar ideas, *i.e.*, by education.

But there is worse to come. Even when our ideas are steadied by habits based on repetitions of impressions, there are ways in which this can happen, or fail to happen, which we nevertheless do not on reflection call probabilities or improbabilities, and which Hume chooses to call "unphilosophical probabilities".

An important question now arises. It is one thing to describe the objects which are respectively called probabilities, improbabilities, prejudices, superstitions, fancies, and so on; in general it is one thing to describe what is called reasonable thinking and what is called unreasonable thinking. But it is another thing to explain and justify the commendatory and derogatory senses in which we always use these terms. What is wrong with the other relations and other habits, and the unphilosophical probabilities?

Hume's way of dealing with this question, in accordance with his "experimental method", is to point out the causes which make us distrust, dislike, and abstain from these mental processes, when we do distrust, dislike, and abstain from them. This, in his view, is a sufficient *explanation* of the derogatory sense in which their names are used. For *justification* he is content, so far as I can see, to rely on the method of challenge ; to challenge anyone not to be influenced by these causes, in the absence of other special counteracting causes, and not to be influenced by the thought of these causes when they are pointed out to him.

We must now try to say what, according to Hume, these causes are, after comparing what he says on this matter in various places.

In Part III, Sect. IX (p. 111), he says of the ideas enlivened by other relations, *i.e.*, contiguity and resemblance, that since, in the absence of a customary or causal connexion with the present impression, we can form the idea of any object we please, and "of our mere goodwill and pleasure give it a particular relation to the impression", and since on the recurrence of the same impression, we need not "place the same object (*i.e.*, idea of an object) in the same relation to it", the mind "from the very first instant feels the looseness of its actions", *i.e.*, does not feel that steadiness and resistance to rival ideas which is essential to what we call belief. Such is the difference between a fancy and a genuine belief.

He goes on to explain (p. 112) how our perception of this difference puts us on our guard against fancies. "As this imperfection (*i.e.*, the "looseness") is very sensible in every single instance, it still increases by experience and observation, when we compare the several instances we may remember, and form a *general rule* against the reposing any assurance in those momentary glimpses of light, which arise in the imagination from a feigned resemblance and contiguity". The essence of the *general rule* is that it is a generalisation from experience to the effect that certain types of lively ideas are not likely to remain firm and steady. Therefore, not expecting them to remain beliefs, we cease to believe them.

His observations on beliefs due to education (p. 118) are similar; experience of the variability, contradictoriness and artificiality of the maxims of educators, as well as of their frequent incompatibility with experience, warns us of instability and inconsistency (*i.e.*, "muddle") to come if we adhere to them. By sticking to experience we can form a consistent and steady picture of the way of the world, including the ways of educators, but by sticking to the teaching of educators we can form no such picture.

In the section "Of Unphilosophical Probability" he deals with various other phenomena on the same lines.

First, the variation in the influence of experiences on our thoughts and actions according to their nearness or remoteness in time. This, he says, we discount in our wiser moments, because otherwise "an argument must have a different force today from what it shall have a month hence". Here again we have a general rule warning us of muddle to come.

Next he considers the fact that a long chain of connected arguments, carrying the mind through a long chain of causes and effects, gives a much less lively persuasion than a direct causal inference.

This fact troubles Hume as a historian; for, if always operative, it should in time destroy our assurance of all the propositions of ancient history, the evidence for which depends on a long series of verbal reports passing through many mouths to the first historians, and a long series of copies and editions of their works, each new copy being an effect of the previous one. But he thinks it is "contrary to commonsense" to suppose that "if the republic of letters and the art of printing continue on the same footing as at present, our posterity can ever doubt that there was such a man as Julius Cæsar".

His solution of the difficulty is that though the links of the argument are innumerable "they are all of the same kind, and depend on the fidelity of copyists". Therefore, "the mind runs easily along them, jumps from one part to another with facility and forms but a general notion of each link".

This solution, though possibly not an altogether false description of the mental processes of the casual reader, does scant justice to those of the critical historian. The latter surely weighs and adds together the possibilities of falsification at each step of the process of tradition, and his belief survives the lengthy chain of evidence, not because the links are similar, but because he knows that unless beliefs do so survive the same argument will have a different force on different occasions, according to the length of the chain of arguments in which it is a link. This would inevitably lead to muddle. It is really a special case of the same argument having a different force at different times, which Hume has already noticed.

Next Hume considers (pp. 146–48) rash generalisations or prejudices, which he also calls "general rules" in a bad sense, and inferences in accordance with imperfect analogies, where the case bears only a superficial resemblance to the previous experiences by which we judge its expected effects.

As instances, he gives the prejudice that no Irishmen are witty, and the fear of falling entertained by a man suspended

at a great height in a strong iron cage. These cases he says are
at bottom of the same kind. In each a certain feature of objects
or situations has often, perhaps always, been associated in a
man's experience with some other feature, which excites some
passion. Irish nationality has been accompanied by dullness in
many cases, great height has been followed by falls. Thus the
man tends to expect dullness in any Irishman, although well-
educated Irishmen are often witty, and a fall, though the iron
cage is an adequate support. The habit formed by the perfectly
resembling cases, the ill-educated Irishmen he has met, the
ill-supported elevations, assisted by the passions of dislike and
fear, run away with his fancy and operate in cases which only
imperfectly resemble them.

Such convictions, Hume says, can only be corrected by
" general rules" in the good sense; "these rules are formed on
the nature of our understanding, and on our experience of its
operations in the judgements we form concerning objects.
By them we learn to distinguish the accidental circumstances
from the efficacious causes". We make some rash generalisation
or inference; "but when we take a review of this act of the mind,
and compare it with the more general and authentic operations
of the understanding, we find it to be of an irregular nature,
and destructive of all the most established principles of
reasoning, which is the cause of our rejecting it". This
correction is not always made; in wise men the general rules
in the good sense prevail, the vulgar are commonly guided by
the bad kind of general rules.

These general rules then are generalisations about the way
our minds work; not generalisations, as far as Hume here
suggests, about the successfulness or the reverse of different
kinds of expectations, but simply about the way our minds
normally work when not influenced by transient passions and
fancies. We do not normally expect a thing of a kind x, which
has often been followed by a consequence of a kind y, to have
that consequence where a feature z is present, which always
has consequences incompatible with y.

If, therefore, I expect to fall from my high position, though
supported by a strong iron cage, my expectation is "irregular",
inconsistent with our general view of things, likely to disappear
when I return to a normal state of mind and likely to be

opposed to the expectations of other normal observers; in short, a source of muddle. This way of thinking cannot give us a steady and consistent picture of the world. The other, the reasonable way, can, and can account for the occurrence of the irregular ways of thinking, as Hume does. Steadiness and consistency of conception is not only a *sine qua non* of genuine belief, but is also what we like,[1] and, therefore, we prefer those operations of the imagination which we find can give it, to those which we find do not.

Finally, we must consider what Hume says in the section "Of Scepticism with regard to Reason".

Here we are told that the mind, having experience of its own liability to prove mistaken, tends to correct all its judgements, both those of relations of ideas, *e.g.*, mathematics, and those of probability and matter of fact, by probable judgements of the chances of its having been mistaken.

Here is a new kind of general rule, a generalisation not about how we normally think, but about the frequencies of success and failure attained by our different mental processes in various circumstances. We run over our calculations again and again, we get them checked by others, we distrust them if we were tired when we made them, and so on. And these reflex judgements themselves require a similar correction, and an estimate of the chances of being mistaken in our estimation of the chances of error in our original inference. The process can be continued *ad libitum*.

Here then is another cause which leads us to prefer "probable" beliefs to fancies, prejudices, and other irrational beliefs; to wit, our experience of their superior reliability.

We can now sum up Hume's account of "rationality" and "irrationality" and his case for being "rational".

Ideas enlivened by other relations, because of the looseness and arbitrary nature of the process, fail to steady our conceptions at all. Ideas inculcated by education are distrusted because they are found to be mutually inconsistent, dependent on variable causes, inconsistent with experience and incapable of giving us a fixed and steady conception of the way of the

---

[1]Steadiness and consistency, freedom from muddle, are according to Hume the objects of a "calm but strong passion", which also plays an important part in forming our moral judgements. (Treatise Book II, Part III, Sect. III; Book III, Part I, Sect. I, and Part III. Sect. I).

world. Variations of assurance due to lapse of time and length
of argument, implying a fluctuation in the force of the same
argument, are a source of inconsistency and instability in our
beliefs. Rash generalisations and faulty analogies are contrary
to our "general rules" about the way the mind normally works,
and so cannot be expected to give us a steady and lasting
conviction. Finally, "reasonable" beliefs are beliefs of the kind
experience shows to be most reliable.

On the whole, therefore, reason, *i.e.*, trust in experience,
gives us that steady, consistent, comprehensive conception of
things which is genuine belief, and which we desire in our fear
of muddle, and gives us also a steady picture of the causes of
muddle. It is the function of habit to steady and fix our ideas;
turning in on itself it accustoms us to expect this steadiness
from some habits rather than others, and so provides a remedy
for its own imperfections.

4. *Scepticism* (Treatise Book I, Part IV, Sect. I)

So far Hume's philosophy presents a hopeful, positive, anti-
sceptical aspect. We have a way of reasoning capable of giving
us a steady and comprehensive set of beliefs stateable partly
in the form of established generalisations without known
exceptions (proofs) and partly of established statistical
frequencies. Of this way of reasoning, since experience shows
it to be reliable, we have no grounds to complain, unless we
make the mistake of demanding logical demonstrations outside
their proper sphere, the relations of ideas.

But in the section "Of Scepticism with regard to Reason"
this cup of comfort is no sooner offered than it is dashed from
our lips. Probable reasoning, we are told (p. 178), is self-
destructive rather than self-confirmatory, and nothing but
inattention, due to the strain of following out its self-destructive
procedure, can save us from total scepticism. Fortunately,
nature has seen to it that we always are so saved.

The argument may be put as follows. We establish, say,
a 99/100 probability for a certain proposition; remembering
that we are always liable to error we examine the probability of
our being right in this estimate; we find it is, say, 999/1000. The
probability of the original proposition sinks to the product of
99/100 and 999/1000, *i.e.*, 98901/100000. Since we are always

liable to be mistaken in any calculation or inference, this process must be repeated *ad infinitum*, and each time the probability will diminish. Hume argues that no probability can subsist under an infinite number of diminutions, and that, had we patience to be ideally reasonable, and to correct all our judgements by estimates of the likelihood of being mistaken, no probabilities would remain at all.

I am not seriously perturbed by this argument. Let us call a judgement which is not about judgements, but about other things, a first-order judgement, and a judgement about the reliability of a first-order judgement a second-order judgement. Now it seems evident to commonsense that the second-order judgement that I am very likely, though not certain, to be correct in some first-order judgement increases rather than diminishes the authority of that first-order judgement. We feel more, not less inclined to believe what Mr. Churchill says, when he reminds us that he has "not always been wrong". Hume himself seems to admit this at the bottom of p. 177.

I suspect that even if the principle of the multiplication of probabilities applies to probability judgements of different orders (which I doubt), the application is complicated by the fact that the higher-order judgements, being based on a much wider range of experiments, in some cases on our whole experience of the workings of the human mind and the progress of science, may give more in added weight to the evidence, than they take away by diminishing the probability fraction; just as, even where first-order judgements only are concerned, we feel more confident of our recovery from a disease on the evidence of very full statistics giving a chance of recovery of 4/5, than we do on the evidence of very meagre statistics showing a chance of recovery of 9/10.[1]

I suggest, therefore, that Hume's sceptical argument can be disregarded as a mistake, and his positive account and recommendation of probable reasoning accepted as in substance

---

[1] I have, throughout the discussion on probability, avoided the very difficult question whether the mere number of favourable cases, independently of the variety of their circumstances, affects the probability of the proposition in support of which they are cited. I think Hume assumes that it does; he certainly thinks it does in the case of unreflective probability judgements, based on habit alone. It is not clear whether he does, or ought to, assume it in the case of reflective probability judgements.

the best that can be offered. This is quite compatible with granting to Hume that *in practice*, for most people, weariness and inattention are a surer defence against sceptical sophistries than are any counter arguments, valid or invalid, which philosophers can devise.

CHAPTER VII

NECESSARY CONNEXION

(Treatise Book I, Part III, Sect. XIV)

1. *The question and the answer*

THE lengthy preparations are now over, and the scene is set for the kill. A lesser writer, exhausted by so many attendant enquiries, and feeling that he had virtually given the answer already, might have allowed the final section on the idea of necessary connexion to fall a little flat. Hume, on the contrary, gives us a section splendid with eloquence, rich in intimations of a philosophical attitude whose possibilities are only now being fully developed, and remorseless in the logic with which he forestalls every possible argument by which the reader may seek to escape the conclusion, which he states again and again in ever more forcible terms.

The question is, what is the impression from which we derive that idea of necessary connexion, which is an essential part of our idea of the relation of cause and effect?

The answer is inevitable, after all that has been said about belief, probability and the way in which we actually come to pronounce one event the cause of another, and infer from the one to the other; and the answer is given on the second page of the section (p. 154).

There is a feeling of being determined by custom to pass from a certain impression to a certain idea. That feeling makes the idea a belief. That same feeling makes us call the event represented an effect and the transition an inference. That same feeling when it continues, supported by fusion of images, after we have surveyed all the relations of likeness and difference between the present case and the rest of our experience, makes us call the inference probable or reasonable. It is this very same feeling which is the impression from which the idea of necessary connexion is derived.

Hume's contention is partly negative; he is denying something which other philosophers, and to a certain extent plain men, have believed in. They have believed that there is either a certain direct relation between certain objects and events, or alternatively a certain quality in certain objects, whose names are "necessary connexion", "power", "agency", "force", "energy", "efficacy", which terms, he says, are nearly synonymous. People think that somewhere in objects there is a quality in virtue of which, when something happens in that object or in that part of it where the quality resides, certain consequences must ensue; much as people think that in certain men, such as Napoleon, there is some quality in virtue of which, if they will or order others to do something, those others do that thing.

How nebulous and unintelligible this notion is in regard to "powerful men" is the theme of the final chapter of Tolstoy's "War and Peace".

Again, some fatalists think that events succeed one another as they do, because they are inscribed on a sort of scroll which is unrolled steadily in the direction that goes from future to past; each event enters the illuminated circle of the present because it is drawn into it by the previous event, now passing into the twilight of the past, and as it comes draws after it its successor on the " scroll of fate".

There is no faintest confirmation in experience for any such supposition, says Hume. Nor would any such quality or relation do the work that we require of it, that is enable us to infer from the observed to the unobserved. What is more capricious than the behaviour of powerful men, or more unpredictable than the waning of their powers? Of what use to us to know that the future is the predetermined sequel of the present, unless we know what order of future events is written on the scroll?

To some minds the laws of nature as conceived in classical physics, Newton's law of gravity for instance, seemed to afford a clear notion of the union of necessary regularity and efficacious powers. Was it not called the force of gravity? Was it not also called the law of gravity?

But *how* do the moon and sun *pull* the tidal waters of the earth? How does the sun *hold* the planets in their orbits? Action at a distance? Exerted through what medium? The notion is far from clear. And what of the necessary regularity? When we look into the grounds of our belief in its necessity we can find nothing but the influence of concealed tautologies[1] and the evidence of experience, which is only experience of regular *movements*.

Hume then denies the existence of any power or agency in objects; his denial is based on what I have called the method of challenge. He says "If any one think proper to refute this assertion, he need not put himself to the trouble of inventing any long reasonings, but may at once show us an instance of a cause where we discover the power or operating principle. This defiance we are obliged frequently to make use of, as being almost the only means of proving a negative in philosophy".

But, someone will say, there may be such a thing, though we cannot observe it. In the Deity, as the Cartesians and Berkeley supposed, or in the unobservable ultimate constituent particles of matter, as Locke supposed, real power may reside.

But this is to miss the force of Hume's challenge. If you are not acquainted with any instance of power in an object, or of anything like it in its essential attributes, then you can have no idea what it is you suppose to be there. You have no model on which to frame your conception, and therefore, unless you lay claim to innate ideas, you cannot have such a conception. "All ideas are derived from and represent impressions. We never have any impression that contains any power or efficacy. We never, therefore, have any idea of power".

Now, as we have seen, according to the underlying implications of Hume's view of impressions and ideas, and of abstract ideas, "To have an idea of power" is to know what "power" means. If we have no idea of power, we do not know what "power" means. It is not, therefore, an intelligible question of fact whether the Deity or atoms have power. It is a meaningless question. "We do not understand our own meaning in talking so" (p. 166).

---

[1] "Every body continues in its state of rest or uniform motion, except in so far as it is compelled by a force to change that state" is a disguised definition of what we mean by "force".

We may choose, Hume says, to call by the name of "power" whatever unknown properties material or immaterial objects may have, and if we do "it will be of little consequence to the world". "But when instead of meaning these unknown qualities, we make the terms of power and efficacy signify something of which we have a clear idea, and which is incompatible with those objects to which we apply it, obscurity and error begin then to take place".

Hume then does deny the existence of any power or necessary connexion *in objects*. The suggestion of it is meaningless. And necessary connexion is an essential element in our idea of a causal relation between objects. Does it then follow, as some have supposed, that Hume denies the existence of relations of cause and effect between objects, and regards such talk as nonsensical?

I do not think it does. It is true that he regards the idea of necessary connexion as an essential part of the idea of a causal relation between objects; but he denies that the idea of a necessary connexion *residing in the objects* is an essential part of our idea of a causal relation between them. On the contrary, he defines the causal relation in terms of temporal succession, spatial contiguity and constant conjunction of the *objects*, plus a customary transition of the *mind*. And the feel of this customary transition is what is expressed by such terms as "necessary connexion", when we call the objects necessarily connected. It is significant and true to say that flame causes heat; but the constituent elements of the relationship are divided, temporal and spatial contiguity and constant conjunction being in the objects, their necessary connexion being something in the mind.

The terms "necessity", "power", etc., refer, therefore, to a felt process in our own minds concerned with our thoughts about objects which we have experienced. Any such term is, therefore, "incompatible with those objects to which we apply it", when we apply it to the purely objective relations and qualities of things, apart from our thought about them, or to objects beyond the reach of our experience. No such objects can possibly correspond to the idea, and that is why philosophers who tried to make them do so found the topic so difficult.

2. *The importance of the answer*

Let us now consider the philosophical importance of Hume's contention. It is important in two ways. First, as a proposed solution of a major philosophical problem; "I have just now examined one of the most sublime questions in philosophy, viz., *that concerning the power and efficacy of causes* where all sciences seem so much interested" (p. 154). Secondly, as a classical example of the right way of solving those problems which admit of philosophical solution. We will consider these two importances in order.

Philosophers in trying to explain the universe were from the earliest times interested in two main questions: What is the universe made of, and how does it work? The second of these is the question of the efficacy of causes. Many tried to find a close connexion between the two questions: If the universe be made of fire, it must work by burning (Heraclitus). If the universe be made of small hard particles or atoms, it must work by the continual falling of these atoms in the void and the movements generated by their collisions (Epicurus, Lucretius). Others, seeing that the processes of burning, falling, and communicating motion by impulse, though common and familiar, were yet unintelligible and required explanation, supposed that the operating principle must be the will or purpose of some mind or minds by which the universe is animated or controlled.

To Plato and Aristotle this last seemed the only intelligible sort of explanation. The Cartesians and Occasionalists also, finding in their conception of matter no suggestion of power or activity, supposed the will of the Deity to be the only true operating principle. Leibnitz and Berkeley went further and maintained that the universe consisted wholly of minds, and consequently worked by the influence of voluntary activity alone.

But in spite of the massing of philosophical opinions on the side of explanation in terms of voluntary purpose, the materialist view continued to appeal to natural scientists, who found much fruitful use for such conceptions as physical energy, attraction, and gravity, however obscure they might be to philosophers.

Each school believed in "power", whether they ascribed it

to matter or to will. Hume's complaint against all these philosophers is expressed on p. 155 of the Treatise.

"Before they entered on these disputes, methinks it would not have been improper to have examined what idea we have of that efficacy, which is the subject of the controversy. This is what I find principally wanting in their reasonings, and what I shall here endeavour to supply".

They did not ask exactly what it was they were looking for, what was the exact meaning of the question. Or rather, if they did ask, they were content with verbal definitions in terms which were merely synonymous, "efficacy", "agency", "power", "force", "energy", "necessity", "connexion", "productive quality".

We are thus led to the importance of Hume's contention as an example of philosophical method.

What we should do, Hume tells us (p. 155), is to search for the idea, not in definitions, "but in the impressions from which it is originally derived". The philosophical question is just what do we mean by certain terms, and the philosophical answer will consist ultimately, not in a formal definition, but in some way of focusing our attention on just those elements of experience with which the words are customarily connected.

"This", a notable modern philosopher[1] may be heard repeatedly to say in the course of a philosophical discussion, "is a *conceptual* investigation". Fires, moving bodies, human wills have power or energy according to the ordinary way of speaking; that is a statement of empirical *fact*. Before asking whether only moving bodies, or only wills *really* have power, which is a metaphysical question, let us ask just what it is about these things that makes us say they have power; this last is a conceptual question. If you wish to maintain that properly or more exactly speaking only wills, or only moving bodies have power, point out to us just what discoverable peculiarities they have, and how these peculiarities make this more exact way of speaking superior to the ordinary way.

So far the matter seems fairly simple. The problem should be no more difficult than that of making clear by stories and examples what is meant by calling a person "kind". But it is

[1]Professor Wittgenstein.

not simple. It has never been a major philosophical question in what persons kindness really resides or in what parts of them. Some peculiar difficulty attends the concept of necessity or power.

What happens is that, though it is natural in the ordinary way of speaking to say that moving bodies have power and that there are necessary connexions between their movements and their collisions, when we examine these objects and events closely we find *nothing* which it seems natural so to describe. Consequently philosophers have been driven to say that the power and necessity must *really* lie elsewhere, in their concealed properties or in the Deity.

This sort of thing goes on, until, having excluded power and necessity from all observable and confined it to unobservable objects, we wonder how we can ever have come by this idea at all, and either conclude that it is an innate idea, whatever that may mean, or that we have no such idea, and that the terms are meaningless. But plainly the terms are *not* meaningless ; they form very useful items in our everyday vocabulary ; and plainly they do not stand for innate ideas, because we use them to mark some differences or other which only experience can discover. Which things and persons have power, and what they have power to do, are empirical questions.

This is the situation that makes this particular "conceptual investigation" both necessary and difficult; and Hume shows his understanding of the nature of the situation in the following passage (pp. 160–61) :—

> "Thus upon the whole we may infer that when we talk of any being . . . as endowed with a power or force . . . ; when we speak of a necessary connexion betwixt objects, and suppose that this connexion depends on an efficacy or energy with which any of these objects are endowed; in all the expressions, *so applied*, we have really no distinct meaning, and make use only of common words, without any clear and determinate ideas. But as it is more probable that these expressions do here lose their true meaning by being *wrong applied*, than that they never have any meaning; it will be proper to bestow another consideration on this subject, to see if possibly we can

discover the nature and origin of those ideas we annex to them".

Hume suggests, in short, that the cause of the trouble is that, through failure to understand the ordinary use of these terms, we have used them in contexts where they have no meaning. The remedy is to clear up the normal use of these terms.

In order to do this Hume repeats arguments he has used before (p. 161 *et seq.*). He describes just what does happen that makes us say that two objects are necessarily connected or that one is the cause of the other; *i.e.*, they are constantly conjoined in experience and we habitually expect the one when we see the other. Since the true use of such terms as " necessity " and "power" is to express this feeling of customary transition (or inference) in the mind, if we try to use them to stand for a purely objective relation between things, it is not surprising that we can find or imagine no such objective relation. It is like looking for effective oratory in the land of the deaf.

This, then, is the lesson of Hume's account of necessary connexion, regarded as an example of philosophical method. Philosophical problems arise through common words, whose common use is insufficiently understood, being "wrong applied"; they are to be solved by examining the common use, and seeing just what applications of the words must be "wrong", or at best misleading.

But there remains one question. Why do we have this very strong tendency to abuse certain words, and why do we find it so difficult to give it up ? Why is Hume's account of necessary connexion so "violent" a paradox, as he admits it to be ? (p. 164).

Hume's answer is, that "the mind has a great propensity to spread itself on external objects, and to conjoin with them any internal impressions which they occasion, and which always make their appearance at the same time that these objects discover themselves to the senses" (p. 165).

Thus, he says, tastes and smells are spoken and thought of as being located in the objects that give rise to them, though properly speaking tastes and smells are not located anywhere. Pleasures and pains, he might have added, are spoken of as if they were qualities of the objects which occasion them. Not only is the apple sweet, it is also "delicious". And in particular, he is going to maintain, those peculiar pleasures and pains which the thought of certain things and human actions and dispositions produces, approval and disapproval, enjoyment and disgust, are spoken of as if they were inherent qualities of the objects, qualities whose names are "right" and "wrong", "good" and "bad", "beautiful" and "ugly".

Hume does not offer any further explanation of this natural propensity of the mind to spread itself on objects. It is just an empirical fact about us.

It is not, we should notice, the same as what is often called the tendency to "anthropomorphic projection"; nor is his account of the idea of causal power the same as that which represents it as an anthropomorphic projection of the feeling of muscular effort or voluntary striving (p. 159). It is not, according to Hume, that by an inadequate analogy we come to ascribe to the wind or to the engine of our car the same experience of striving and muscular effort which we feel when we blow or pull; though I think we do actually tend to do this. It is that we mistake our own inference, the habitual compulsion which we feel to pass from belief in one proposition to belief in another, for a quality in things compelling a transition in fact from the state of affairs described by one proposition to the state of affairs described by the other.

It is a difficult question whether this tendency is the cause or the effect of the device of language by which we use terms such as "produce", "necessitate", "must follow", "force", etc., as grammatical predicates of the objects of which we speak, although their real purpose is to express our internal impression. It is certain, I think, that this trick of language has fortified metaphysicians in adhering to the errors Hume exposes; and it is not difficult to suggest an explanation of this trick of language based on facts which Hume himself notices.

Were we content to express merely the sentiments of the moment as they originally arise in the soul, we should no doubt need for the purpose only expletives and verbs such as like, dislike, love, hate, etc. But, as Hume is at pains to point out in respect of the sentiments both of belief and moral approval, in order to avoid the inconveniences of constant muddle and conflict both with ourselves and others, we regulate and correct our sentiments by "general rules". We, therefore, require special terms for the expression of these corrected sentiments. Thus belief which is confined, irrespective of other considerations, to what is very or exactly like what has invariably or often happened, requires a special form of expression. And so does approval confined to the sort of action which in nearly all cases brings pleasant consequences to most people concerned, irrespective of the particular interests of the speaker in the present case. Since these corrected sentiments depend on the answers to factual questions (is this like what has always happened? does this usually lead to consequences most human beings like? etc.), it is natural to express them in the form of statements of objective fact, "this is probable", or "this is a necessary consequence of x", or "that act is right".

3. *Objections to Hume's answer*

There are, I think, only three objections of any weight that can be brought against Hume's account. All of them are answered by Hume himself.

The first is that causes operate whether we are thinking of them or not; but, according to Hume's view, necessity, an essential element in the causal relation, lies in our thought about the objects, not in the objects.

Hume's answer is simple (p. 166). Regularity of succession is, we find, a real property of objects. We have no reason to doubt that heated metals do in fact expand when we are not observing them, just as much as when we are. But if we ascribe more than regularity to the objects, we are talking nonsense. I do not think the modern scientist would complain of this answer. He claims to describe "operations of nature which are independent of our thought and reasoning". But he does not claim to do more than describe them. He does not claim to *explain* them by reference to any secret inherent powers and necessities.

The second objection is that Hume's account is circular; he defines the necessary connexion of objects in terms of a necessary connexion in the mind between an impression and an associated lively idea. Or, to put it another way, his account is self-contradictory. He says that necessity is not to be found anywhere in nature, "neither in superior nor inferior natures, neither in body nor in spirit". But he also says that "necessity is something that exists in the mind" (p. 163).

Hume's answer to this objection is given in a paragraph at the bottom of p. 166 and the top of p. 167, in which he explains exactly in what sense necessity is in the mind.

Before considering this passage it is worth pointing out that Hume's usual word for the internal impression from which the idea of necessity is derived is "determination", which lends colour to the objection. This word, however, is not included in the list of words he gives on p. 155 as synonyms for "power" and "necessity". It is true that he does on p. 110 of the *Treatise* speak of the mind as feeling itself "*necessarily* determined to view these particular ideas". It is clear, I think, what Hume means in that passage by " necessary". "Determined" means, as often elsewhere, "determined by custom". When he says that custom necessarily determines us to view a particular idea, he means that that particular idea succeeds the impression with the peculiar facility, the felt familiar click which is characteristic of any habitual action,[1] and that no other idea does; custom thus ties us down to that particular idea; and in this sense it is "necessary" to form this particular idea rather than any other. Hume also uses the phrase "necessarily determined" of our assent to intuitive and demonstrative propositions (p. 97). Here again he means that the mind can only conceive one idea in a certain way and cannot conceive incompatible ideas in that way; but in this case it is tied down, not by custom, but by the inconceivability, *i.e.*, self-contradictoriness of all incompatible ideas. They cannot be conceived clearly.

Let us now consider the passage on pp 166 and 167; though it can scarcely be improved upon, I will give a free paraphrase.

I receive an impression of, say, a flame, and feel determined to form a lively idea of heat. It is this feeling of determination which I refer to when I say that the flame and the heat are necessarily connected. Now the objection to be considered says that this determination is itself a necessary connexion between

---

[1] This feeling is experienced every day in such actions as tying a shoe-lace, changing gear on a car, making a correct citation from a multiplication table or a familiar poem, or spelling a word correctly.

the impression of flame and the idea of heat; so that one necessary connexion is merely substituted for another.

Hume's answer is that there is no such substitution in his account. It is a true proposition that flame is necessarily connected with heat. But this proposition does not *mean* that the impression of flame is necessarily connected with the idea of heat. It simply expresses the feeling of customary transition from the impression to the idea, and asserts the constant conjunction of flame and heat. It is *also* a true proposition that the impression of flame causes, and is, therefore, necessarily connected with, the idea of heat. This second proposition asserts *another* constant conjunction, between the impression and the idea, and expresses *another* felt determination of the mind, *i.e.*, the customary feeling of the transition from the experience of having an impression of a flame to the expectation of forming an idea of heat. At whatever level of reflexion we predicate a necessary connexion, we are never asserting more than constant conjunction of the objects we speak of, and are always expressing a customary facility in the transition of our thoughts about them. And this holds good even when we are thinking about our thoughts.

There is here no such vicious infinite regress as, for instance, Professor Whitehead[1] thinks. Hume is not saying that the necessary connexion between flame and heat consists in a necessary connexion between our impression of flame and our idea of heat, and that that necessary connexion consists in a necessary connexion between the thought of an impression of flame, and the thought of an idea of heat, and so on. That would indeed be a vicious infinite regress. He makes clear that each time we say "necessary connexion", we express a new feeling of determination. The necessary connexion between flame and heat is the feeling attending the transition from the impression of flame to the idea of heat. The necessary connexion between the impression of flame and the idea of heat is the new feeling attending the transition from the thought of an impression of flame to that of an idea of heat. The two feelings are separate entities, and the two necessary connexions are two distinct necessary connexions. The former is not identified with the

[1]"Process and Reality", p. 196. For defence of Hume, compare John Laird "Hume's Philosophy of Human Nature", p. 128.

latter, nor even defined in terms of it. The necessary connexion between the flame and the heat is defined in terms of the feeling attending our thoughts about them. The necessary connexion between our thoughts about them is something different, and is defined in terms of the feeling attending our thoughts about those thoughts.

You can, of course, go on reflecting, and reflecting about your reflexions and reflecting about your reflexions about your reflexions, and so on, as long as you please. But wasting your time in this way does not convict Hume of a vicious infinite regress.

The third principal objection is considered by Hume on p. 159 of the Treatise, and much more fully in the Enquiry, Sect. V, Part II, paras. 51–53. This objection is that though external objects give us no idea of power or necessary connexion, we have an internal impression of it, and are every moment conscious of the power of the will over the movements of the body and the processes of the mind. Hume denies that we have any such consciousness.

In the fuller treatment in the Enquiry he makes three points with regard to the power of the will over the body.

First, so far from the influence of mind on body being something of which we are intimately conscious, it is one of the most mysterious principles in nature and quite beyond our comprehension. We cannot understand how unextended mind, which is either a spiritual substance or not a substance at all, is able "to actuate the grossest matter". Were we intimately conscious of this power of the will over the body, we must know it; we should know and understand how mind actuates matter, and it would not be the inexplicable philosophical conundrum that it is.

I do not find this argument very convincing. It is perfectly conceivable that we may really be aware of something unique, which is inexplicable and mysterious in that, being unique and unlike anything else, it cannot be explained by means of any general concepts or laws which occur in any scientific or philosophical system. Nevertheless, Hume may be right in thinking that this unique something, if we are aware of it, does not answer to our idea of necessary connexion; and this follows, I think, from his second argument.

His second argument is that it is only by experience that we find out which parts of our body are under the control of the will, and when they are. It is not by being conscious of a lack of some peculiar quality in my volition to move my ears, or my leg when it has "gone to sleep", that I learn that I lack the "power to do so". It is simply by finding that the willed movement does not in fact follow in these cases. There would be no need of these experiments, Hume argues, if I could tell by mere inspection, which of my volitions had efficacious power and which had not. From this it follows that, whatever unique qualities we may be aware of in our volitions, none of them is "power" in the sense required; for they may be present in the volition, and yet the willed movement may not follow. The will may be powerless, and only by trying and seeing can we discover if it is.

This third argument is that "we learn by anatomy" that the immediate effect of successful volition is not the movement of the arm or finger of which we are conscious, but certain changes in the "muscles and nerves and animal spirits, and, perhaps, something still more minute and more unknown"; changes, that is, of which we are *not* conscious. We cannot then be directly aware of a necessary connexion between two events, of one of which we are not conscious at all.

I find both these two arguments unanswerable.

Hume then proceeds to point out that similar arguments apply to the power of the will over the ideas of the imagination; particularly the second argument. We have not always the same command over our ideas; sometimes, as when we cannot remember something, an idea refuses to obey the summons of the will; sometimes an idea refuses to be banished from the mind. Only by trying and seeing can we tell when such volitions are effective.

I conclude then that in its broad outlines at least Hume's conclusion about necessary connexion is inescapable. "The necessary connexion depends on the inference" rather than *vice versa*. "The necessary connexion . . . is the foundation of our inference . . . the foundation of our inference is the transition arising from the accustomed union. These, therefore, are the same". Flame has the *power* to produce heat, heat *must* attend flame. If there is a flame heat *necessarily* follows. The force of all these words is to express an inference, or a readiness to make an inference; perhaps also, though this Hume did not consider, to recommend the inference, or to commit ourselves to it. Inferences are made, or at least only adhered to, approved of, recommended, accepted, in cases where there is either a logical relation of ideas, *i.e.* a connexion of meaning, or a constant conjunction in experience such as Hume describes, or something like it. They are never founded on an insight into some real necessitation in the nature of things.

CHAPTER VIII

BODIES

(Treatise Book I, Part IV, Sects. II and IV)

1. *The problem*

HUME'S views on our belief in the existence of material objects
(and the same is true of his account of the self) are far more
sceptical and far less convincing than any of his contentions
that we have hitherto examined, except his mistaken theory
of the self-destructiveness in theory of probable reasoning.

Philosophers have always been perplexed by an acute
difficulty about our knowledge of the material world.

It is by the sensations we get that we decide questions about
material things ; remove these sensations and we should know
nothing of them. But when we ask what are the relations
between our sensations and material things which enable the
former to serve as the touchstone of truth with regard to the
latter, we encounter difficulties.

Reflection shows that our sensations are very different in
kind from the material things we believe to exist. They are
interrupted where the material things are believed to be per-
sistent, they are dependent as to their qualities and their
existence on our wills[1] where the material things are believed to
be independent, they alter where the material things are believed
to remain unchanged.

Scientific investigations, based on a primary acceptance of
the evidence of the senses, re-emphasise and increase these
differences. All the sensible qualities by which our sensations
are differentiated and characterised are found to be due to our
own constitutions, subjective effects of material causes. Colour,
warmth, hardness, noise, smell, like aches and pains and tastes,
are found to be nothing in the objects ; remove the conscious

---

[1] *i.e.* on our voluntary movements.

observer and they would vanish away. They are therefore called "secondary" qualities. The "primary" qualities remaining to the object are shape, size, position, motion and the like, the list varying from time to time according to the current scientific theories. Even the primary qualities of shape, size and motion are very different from the apparent shapes, sizes and motions directly revealed to us in sense-experience. The developments of modern physics have done nothing to diminish the difference.

Finally, as Descartes pointed out, there is an absolute absence of any logical connexion between sensations and material objects. Not only is it conceivable that there should be material things but no sensations (which would happen if there were no living things), but it is also conceivable that there should be sensations, or occurrences indistinguishable from them, but no material things. Dreams and hallucinations illustrate this possibility. Why should not all our experience be a dream, a mere magic-lantern show contrived by an all-powerful arch-deceiver ?

The question arises, how do we nevertheless form conclusions about material things on the evidence of our senses, and form them with such complete assurance that for most of our everyday waking lives we scarcely distinguish the material object from its sensible appearances ?

Philosophers have offered three main types of answer :—

(i) The mystical answer. The material world suggested by sense is an illusion. There is within it no step from "It seems to me" to "It is". Reality, as distinct from appearance, is wholly non-material, consisting either solely of spirits, or of spirits and objects that are intelligible but not sensible. This is the answer found in much of Plato's writings, in the Hindu philosophy of "Maya", and in Christian Science.

(ii) The rationalist answer. Besides the ideas derived from the senses and retained in the imagination, we have ideas of another kind derived from another source ; purely intellectual concepts, such as substance, cause, and the concepts of pure mathematics, the power of forming which is an innate gift from the Creator. By means of these ideas we can reason out what the external world must be like in order for us to receive the sensations we do receive. The validity of these innate ideas is proved from the veracity of God. The idea of a perfect, and therefore non-deceiving God, is itself an innate idea containing in itself the logical necessity of the real existence of its object, as set out in the ontological argument (see Ch. V). This was the answer of Descartes.

(iii) The phenomenalist answer. There are no innate ideas ; all our ideas are derived from experience, and consequently all our knowledge. We can therefore form no idea of a material world absolutely distinct from sensible appearances ; if we could it would not help to explain our sense-experiences, since the interaction of mind and matter, thus absolutely conceived, is admitted to be inexplicable ; since we cannot form the idea of such a material world, the supposition of its existence is nonsensical, and the question of its truth simply does not arise. It does not, however, follow that the sensible world is a mere illusion, as the mystics said. Within it the distinctions between reality and illusion, object and appearance, hold good. A real thing is a class of sense-experiences that occur, or would occur given the appropriate sensory context, according to settled rules, and for any mind fulfilling the conditions of those rules. The appearances are the individual sense-experiences that are members of the class, and apparent qualities those predicable of the individual members but not of the class. Delusions are experiences confined to certain individual minds and occurring according to different kinds of rules, or no rules at all. The thing therefore is the class of its appearances, the nature of the thing is the rules according to which its appearances occur, and the general rules according to which all appearances occur are the "laws of nature". These rules are learned from experience, and are all that the natural scientist can discover. There is no explanation of the rules of the order of appearances except the will of God. This was the view of Bishop Berkeley.

According to Berkeley there were two prevalent errors to be avoided : (a) The error of "the vulgar", who, identifying things with their sensible appearances, yet suppose these appearances (sounds, colours, etc.) to exist unperceived in the same sense of "exist" as they exist when perceived. This he says is wrong. Unperceived sensible objects exist only in the hypothetical sense that they *could be* perceived, or in some different and to us unknown manner in the mind of God. As known to us, they are permanent possibilities of sensation. (b) The error of the scientists ("the philosophical system" as Hume calls it), who think that they can explain, not merely describe, the order of appearances, in terms of material substances conceived as distinct and different from the appearances, and as causes of them.

Now Hume was plainly too wedded to commonsense and experience to have any truck with the mystical answer. Having rejected innate ideas he could have no use for the rationalist answer. It is his attitude to the phenomenalist answer that is interesting.

Though Hume accepts Berkeley's refutation of "the philosophical system" as unintelligible, and reinforces his arguments in a masterful manner in his section "On the Modern Philosophy", he rejects Berkeley's phenomenalist solution of the problem.

Why does Hume reject this view, the view of a fellow empiricist, whose philosophy is based on much the same empiricist account of meaning as his own, and on an account of abstract ideas which he hails as a momentous discovery; a view apparently so much in keeping with his own general principles, and not in its essentials incompatible with his views on the self, or with his official views on our reasons for belief in God as the artificer of nature?

The clue is to be found in Hume's statement in a footnote to para. 122 of the Enquiry: "That all his (sc. Berkeley's) arguments, though otherwise intended are, in reality, merely sceptical, appears from this, *that they admit of no answer and produce no conviction.* Their only effect is to cause that momentary amazement and irresolution and confusion, which is the result of scepticism".

He does not agree then that Berkeley's view is in accordance with common sense; the vulgar conviction of the permanent existence of the very shapes, colours, etc. we perceive cannot be corrected, as Berkeley thought; we do not "really mean" permanent possibilities of sensation, and we cannot school ourselves to do so. What Berkeley is trying to do, Hume thinks, is to destroy a natural conviction, because it is not clearly intelligible or demonstrable by reason, and to substitute for it a different conviction which is. He is trying to prove that there are no material objects in the ordinary sense of the word. This is a pointless enterprise, and bound to fail.

We cannot, Hume thinks, throw off the natural conviction, however confused it may be, however contradictory to other natural convictions; all that we can do as philosophers is to examine the nature and causes of this natural conviction. He says, "Nature has not left this (*sc.* assent to the principle concerning the existence of body) to his (*sc.* man's) choice, and has doubtless esteemed it an affair of too great importance to be trusted to our uncertain reasonings and speculations. We may well ask, *what causes induce us to believe in the existence of body*? but it is in vain to ask, *whether there be body or not*? That is a point we must take for granted in all our reasonings" (Treatise Book I, Part IV, Sect. II, pp. 182–83).

I wish to maintain three things. First, that Hume was right in maintaining that Berkeley's solution was impossibly para-doxical. Secondly, that Hume's own psychological account of the causes which induce us to believe in the existence of bodies is unconvincing. Thirdly, that he nevertheless puts his finger on certain features of those impressions which we take to be impressions of external objects, which are just the features which we in fact use as criteria for distinguishing the external or physical from the internal or mental[1]; that these features, which Hume calls "constancy" and "coherence", were not noticed by Berkeley, and that if he had noticed them he could have made his phenomenalist solution less paradoxical, though still not wholly satisfactory.

2. *Hume's "solution"*

Hume first says that neither the senses nor reason can pro-duce our belief in the distinct and continued existence of bodies.

The impressions of sense are interrupted, and do not show us either real objects distinct from their sensible appearances, or sensible objects distinct from the self that perceives them. They simply show us themselves as they are. Moreover, the senses reveal no difference of status between colour, shape, hardness, sound, smell, pleasure and pain, and the emotions; they are all originally on the same footing. Yet for some reason we attribute a distinct existence to some of these and not to

---

[1] Sometimes it is used to distinguish, within the "mental", the "conscious" from the "unconscious".

others, and opinions vary as to where to draw the line; particularly with regard to colour, for instance.

As to reason, it is not in fact used to arrive at this conviction. It is not by the arguments which any philosophers may produce that "children, peasants and the greatest part of mankind are induced to attribute objects to some impressions, and deny them to others". Nor can reason possibly be used successfully to justify this conviction. If we do not distinguish between impressions and objects there is no place for inference from one to the other. If we do distinguish them, we cannot infer from the existence of an impression to the existence of an object, since we only observe the impressions, never the objects, and consequently cannot observe any constant conjunctions between impressions and objects, the only possible foundation for an inference from the one to the other (p. 204).

Hume then concludes that since neither sense nor reason persuades us of the distinct and continued existence of body, it must be imagination. Some features of certain of our impressions must work on the imagination to produce this result, since we do not attribute distinct existence to all our impressions.

What are these features? Not, as Berkeley had suggested, involuntariness or superior force or violence. For these are shared by impressions of pain and pleasure and our passions and affections, which we regard as purely subjective. It is two features, which he calls *constancy* and *coherence*.

Impressions of "unchanging objects", such a mountains, houses and trees are *constant*. "They have always appeared to me in the same order; and when I lose sight of them by shutting my eyes or turning my head, I soon after find them return on me without the least alteration".

Where objects to which we attribute an external existence change, they exhibit what he calls *coherence*. This does not merely mean that they change in a regular manner; but that they change in the same manner whether I keep my eye on them or not. "When I return to my chamber after an hour's absence I find not my fire in the same situation in which I left it; but then I am accustomed, in other instances, to see a like alteration produced in a like time, whether I am present or absent, near or remote" (p. 189).

This coherence is different from the regularity found in "those internal impressions, which we regard as fleeting and perishing". "Our passions are found by experience to have a mutual connexion with and dependence on each other; but on no occasion is it necessary to suppose that they have existed and operated, when they were not perceived, in order to preserve the same dependence and connexion of which we have had experience.[1] . . . External objects on the contrary require a continued existence, or otherwise lose, in a great measure, the regularity of their operation" (p. 190). This difference Berkeley failed to notice.

It is important to be quite clear just what this feature of certain experiences which Hume calls "coherence" is. If I sit and watch my fire, I get a series of visual impressions whose size and brightness diminishes in a certain manner at a certain sensible rate. If I sit and watch the clock I get a continuous series of visual impressions of the hands in successive positions which follow on one another at a certain sensible rate. If I arrange things so that I can see both at once, I find the two series of impressions always keep in step with one another; the fire dies down a certain amount while the clock's hands move from 2 p.m. to 3 p.m. I further find that if I look at the clock and the fire alternately or at invervals however chosen, the relations between the occasional impressions of the clock and the fire are just the same as those between similar impressions which formed parts of the two continuous series, which I got when I observed both continuously.

Let us represent the series of impressions I call the fire by capital letters, and those I call the clock by small letters. Then when I observe both continuously I get

(I)   A   B   C   D   E   F, etc.
      a   b   c   d   e   f, etc.

When my observations are interrupted I get series of the following kinds

(II)   A   .   .   D   .   F
       a   .   .   d   .   f

---

[1] This is exactly what Freud has since found it necessary to suppose.

or

	(III)	.	B	.	.	E	.
		a	.	c	.	e	f

or

	(IV)	A	.	.	.	.	F
		.	b	.	.	.	f

and so on.

I never get

	(V)	A	F	.	.	C	B
		a	f	.	.	c	b

or

	(VI)	B	C	.	A	.	E
		a	.	b	.	f	e

To use, with modification, a terminology introduced by Professor Price in "Hume's Theory of the External World", the order of each series and the correlation of the two are "gap-indifferent", that is independent of the size and distribution of the gaps. Whether they are also independent of the kind of other impressions which fill the gaps, I shall consider later.

Now according to Hume, the uniformity of the uninterrupted series (I), and their constant correlation leads me to expect that fires will always die down in the same manner and keep step with the progress of the hands of the clock. But the frequent and often lengthy gaps in the interrupted series (II), (III), (IV) destroy this regularity, and give rise to an opposite expectation that they won't. This uneasiness or contradiction is resolved by an expedient suggested by the gap-indifference of the order and correlation of the two series; I suppose that the gaps are only apparent, and that the missing members really occurred, but were not perceived by me. With the gaps thus filled in series (II), (III), (IV) become the same as series (I).

But Hume cannot rest content with this explanation; it represents my mental processes as being much more self-conscious and rational than they in fact are in ordinary sense perception. Moreover, it is not in accordance with his account of factual beliefs as due to mental habits set up by experienced regularity. According to that account we should simply expect just that degree and kind of regularity which we in fact find in our actual impressions. But here we seem to be demanding a more complete regularity than we in fact find, and introducing a hypothesis or supposition to ensure it. "It is impossible", he says, "that any habit should ever exceed that degree of regularity" which we find in our impressions (p. 191).

He is consequently driven to give a rather lame psychological account of what makes us form this supposition (p. 192). "The imagination, when set into any train of thinking, is apt to continue, even when its object fails it, and, like a galley put in motion by the oars, carries on its course without any new impulse". Consequently, "as the mind is once in a train of observing a uniformity among objects, it naturally continues till it renders the uniformity as complete as possible. The simple supposition of their continued existence suffices for this purpose, and gives us a notion of a much greater regularity among objects, than what they have when we look no further than our senses".

Hume, however, does not think even this principle strong enough to support "so vast an edifice" as our conception of the material world. To reinforce it, he produces another and equally unconvincing psychological explanation based on the influence of "constancy", which he regards as stronger and more fundamental.

The close resemblance of our interrupted impressions of mountains, houses, the sea, etc., makes us forget the interruptions and ascribe an identity to them. We mistake an interrupted series of resembling impressions for a single continuous impression, and form a habit of regarding them as such. Then, when our attention is drawn to the interruptions we see this to be contrary to their supposed identity. Again we feel a conflict in our minds and resolve it by the supposition of continuous unobserved existence, which supposition acquires force and vivacity from the actual impressions we get and our original tendency to regard them as identical, and so becomes a belief (p. 193).

This, according to Hume, is the nature, and these are the causes, of our commonsense conviction of the continued and distinct existence of bodies. It is an imaginative supposition of unperceived impressions, unseen colours and shapes, unfelt textures, pressures and temperatures, unheard sounds, and so on. The supposition is suggested by the "constancy" and "coherence" of some impressions and converted into a belief by its association with those impressions.

This conviction, though natural and indestructible, he goes on to say, is on reflection unsatisfactory to our reason; but not, as Berkeley had said, because the notion of an "unperceived perception" is self-contradictory. For according to Hume, the mind is nothing but a bundle of perceptions, and it is, therefore, quite conceivable that individual perceptions should exist outside the bundle. Being perceived simply means being in the bundle; such perceptions would, therefore, be unperceived (p. 200). The conviction is unsatisfactory because the inductive generalisations which we proceed to make, on the assumption of the continued and distinct existence of bodies, include well-supported beliefs in the dependence of all our perceptions "on our organs and the disposition of our nerves and animal spirits". Such experiments as double-vision, perspectival distortion, illusions due to disease, and so on, show that "our sense perceptions are not possessed of any distinct and independent existence". The progress of our beliefs about the material world thus turns round and, in its later developments, destroys its own foundations.

What Hume is here drawing attention to is the self-contradictoriness of the position of the simple-minded physiologist who says that his *observations by his senses* of human sense organs and human reports of sense-experience, prove that all our sense-experiences are subjective, mere appearances due to physical causes. Such a physiologist plainly cuts off the branch he is sitting on.

But, says Hume, our natural conviction of the independent existence of bodies is too strong to be given up, even though it leads to self-contradictory consequences. Plain men just ignore the difficulty. Scientists seek to remove the contradiction by adopting "the philosophical system". They "distinguish between perceptions and objects, of which the former are supposed to be interrupted and perishing, and different at every different return, the latter to be uninterrupted, and to preserve a continued existence and identity".

This system, which owes all its plausibility to the strength of the vulgar conviction of the permanent and independent existence of bodies, is incomprehensible, as shown in the section "Of the Modern Philosophy". It necessitates stripping matter of all its sensible qualities, since these are dependent on subjective conditions and vary with them. When these are taken away matter consists of mere shape, size and motion, with nothing left that moves or occupies space, and space itself without colour or temperature an inconceivable abstraction. "Impenetrability" does not help; this notion involves two bodies at least, each excluding the other from the space it occupies. But this cannot be conceived, unless each body can be conceived separately; and without sensible qualities they cannot be so conceived; they are mere nonentities, and "two nonentities cannot exclude each other from their places" (p. 219).

Hume concludes (p. 221) "Thus there is a direct and total opposition betwixt our reason and our senses; or more properly speaking, betwixt those conclusions we form from cause and effect, and those that persuade us of the continued and independent existence of body. When we reason from cause and effect, we conclude that neither colour, sound, taste, nor smell have a continued and independent existence. When we exclude these sensible qualities, there remains nothing in the universe which has such an existence".

3. *Criticism of Hume's "solution"*

This is a most unsatisfactory conclusion, and it is difficult to regard it with the complacency which Hume professes to achieve. It is worse than the Berkeleian paradox. Let us therefore examine Hume's account of our belief in material things from the phenomenalist point of view, and see if a solution can be suggested which is less paradoxical than Berkeley's, and less defeatist than Hume's.

Now it seems to me that "constancy" and "coherence" are just the features of experiences which we accept as criteria for regarding them as appearances of independently existing objects. Constancy, I suggest, is simply a special case of coherence. Series of impressions of mountains and seas, however interrupted, preserve the same gap-indifferent correlations with one another and with other series; they also have the peculiarity that the differences between the members of each such series are slight.[1]

But it also seems to me true that the independent existence of certain objects is something we learn by experience, not an ingenious supposition we devise to explain certain contradictions. A child learns that its mother, its cot, its toys are permanent and independent objects by discovering constant correlations in its experience. It does not first observe these correlations and then think of a supposition to explain them. I suggest that what we so learn is to make and apply a number of generalisations from experience. It is the way we symbolise these conclusions in the imagination and the way we find it convenient to express them in language which has given rise to the philosophical difficulties.

Let us take Hume's instance of the fire. My series of impressions of it is either continuous and of a certain kind, or interrupted. When interrupted it may be interrupted in various ways. The gaps may have various different kinds of filling and various sensible contexts.

It may be interrupted by the experiences I call closing my eyes or turning my head, or walking out of the room; or by "something getting between me and it", i.e., by some opaque visual impression of lesser visual depth occupying the same position in my visual field. With regard to gaps so occasioned and so filled the series is gap-indifferent both in its order and its correlations with other series; let us call such gaps "phenomenal gaps".

On the other hand, the series may be interrupted by experiences such as I call somebody throwing a bucket of water on the fire, my wife removing it bodily in a coal-scuttle to the kitchen stove, or, in the case of an electric fire, somebody turning off the switch. With regard to such interruptions, the series is not gap-indifferent. When the fire is relit the correlations with the warmth of the room, the crackling sounds, and the clock are different from what they would have been if the

---

[1] "Constant" series have a special and fundamental importance, but it is not what Hume thought. It is that they provide us with fixed landmarks which we take as frames of reference for the mapping out of objects in physical space. Cf. A. J. Ayer, "Foundations of Empirical Knowledge" ch. V, Sect. 23.

interruption had not occurred. Let us call such gaps "substantial gaps".[1]

Exactly the same distinction applies to those impressions which Hume calls "constant". The series of my impressions of the house across the road is gap-indifferent with regard to gaps caused by my looking away or leaving the neighbourhood. It is not gap-indifferent with regard to gaps caused by bombs, earthquakes, etc. That this distinction is the operative one in both "constancy" and "coherence" is implied by Hume's own words. "When I lose sight of them (sc. the mountains, houses and trees) by shutting my eyes or turning my head, I soon after find them return upon me without the least alteration". Of the "coherence" of the fire he says "I am accustomed . . . to see a like alteration produced in a like time, whether I am present or absent, near or remote'.

Now after I have learned from observation what sort of experiences are usually associated with gaps of these two kinds I am surely entitled, by a straight inductive inference, when a phenomenal gap occurs, to infer that it would not have occurred, if the gap-making experience had not occurred, provided no other gap-making experience occurred instead. I look away, and no longer see the fire. If I had not looked away, experience teaches, I should still be seeing the fire provided no one had switched it off. If I had not turned my gaze from the clock to the fire, provided the clock had not stopped, I should still be seeing the hands of the clock slowly moving on. So I come to think of the missing members of these series as experiences I would have had, if my experience had been in certain ways different from what it in fact was. They are unfulfilled possibilities.

Now, in most cases, it is important to distinguish between what actually happened and what might have happened, or would have happened if something had been different. It is important to distinguish between the opportunity that was taken and the opportunity that was missed, the bet that was won and the bet that was lost, the disaster that occurred and the disaster that was avoided. Nevertheless, it is a familiar fact that we often forget to do so; we find ourselves planning in our

---

[1]This term is not intended to carry any metaphysical implications about "substance" in Locke's sense.

imagination the spending of the sum we would have had if our horse had won, the life we would have led if we had obtained the appointment we lost. It is easy to live in dreams of what might have been. And it is dangerous.

Let us now enquire why we tend to do this, apart from the influence of wishes and fears. Suppose the horse I backed really won. I represent in my imagination what happened on the course; the colours flashing past the post, with mine in front, the cheering crowds, my horse being led in, the bookmaker handing the money to the friend who made the bet for me. Now suppose the horse lost. I represent in my imagination what would have happened if he had won; exactly the same picture.

The imagination can depict no difference between possibilities, whether unfulfilled or undecided, and actualities. In cases where the distinction is important we mark it by a difference in verbal symbols. This picture we remind ourselves, if we are wise, is "what would have happened"; that picture is "what actually happened".

Now in the case of a "substantial gap" in a series such as we have been considering, it is important to remember that the missing members are mere unfulfilled possibilities. The fire, which I would have seen if it had not been extinguished, is no more use for drying clothes than the money, which I would have won if I had not lost my bet, is for buying champagne. But in the case of a "phenomenal gap" it is rarely of any importance at all. Whether I saw the fire, or whether I would have seen it had I looked, the room grows warm, the clothes dry, the crackling sounds occur, and later impressions of the fire, if they occur, will be smaller and less bright. There is no need in this case to distinguish between the impressions I would have had, and those I actually had. It is rarely of any practical importance. So I call them both indifferently "the fire", and in any case must represent them in my imagination by the same picture.

No wonder that a distinction that is not usually marked in thought by a difference in terminology, and cannot be marked by a difference in imagery, comes to be forgotten. Whether we see the fire, or whether we believe we would have seen it if we had looked, we say "there is a fire", "the fire warms the room". *In this sense* there is a fire whether we see it or not, *i.e.*, the phrase "There is a fire" is a true and proper description of the state of affairs alike in the case where we have the sense-impressions and in the case where we have not, but could have had them.

Thus we come to think of "the fire" as the name of an object that exists whether we are aware of it or not, and of which the image, which represents either an actual or a possible view of a fire indifferently, is a picture. We still cling to this opinion, even when for some special reason we ask ourselves whether we did actually have the sense impression or not. And as the answer to this question is often that we did not, we come to think of the impression and the fire as two distinct entities, either of which may exist without the other, in the same sense of the word "exist".

We can now see just why we attribute a distinct and continued existence to some of our impressions and not to others.

The pain which I feel whenever I put my hand too close to the fire is a "permanent possibility of sensation", just as much as the shape and colour I see whenever I look at the fire. But the gaps in the series of the pains are not genuine "phenomenal gaps". Although the conditions in which they occur are similar to those in which phenomenal gaps occur (*i.e.*, they depend on what I call movements of my body), the effects are very different. Whether I jump and scream depends on whether I actually feel the pain or not; nothing depends merely on whether I would feel the pain if I put my hand in the fire.

This point was not noticed by Berkeley, and has been ignored by many other phenomenalists. Hume puts it quite clearly in his statement, "Whenever we infer the continued existence of the objects of sense from their coherence, it is in order to bestow on the objects a greater regularity than what is observed in our mere perceptions" (p. 191).

The distinction of primary and secondary qualities is merely an extension of the same principle. We find that it is not on the colour or warmth of the obtainable impressions that other possibilities of sensation depend, but on their shape, size and position. It is not, therefore, necessary to attribute distinct and continued existence to colour and warmth. Moreover, it is not on the "apparent" sizes and shapes that the most precise consequences depend, but on the measured sizes and shapes; these, therefore, alone are "real".

Now this account which I have given is, I think, still the same in essence as Berkeley's, despite the amendment I have made. "There is a fire" describes either the case in which I see the fire or the case in which I could have seen it (had I looked) but do not. What is common to both these cases is that the sense-impressions are obtainable in certain ways, whether they are actually obtained or not. A material thing is a kind of permanent possibility of sense experiences, which may or may not be fulfilled.

Hume was right in thinking that there are natural impediments to accepting this account. And I have tried to show what one of them is; it lies in the way we symbolise these possibilities in the imagination and in language. But I, for one, do not find this impediment insuperable, once I have understood its nature. There are, however, more serious impediments, for instance the following.[1] Not only is it conceivable that material things might have existed with no minds to perceive them, but geologists tend to say they once did. They describe such things as a land-bridge between Europe and America before there was life on the planet. The Bible tells us that God created the material world before the animals and men. What, on the phenomenalist view, is the meaning of such assertions ? It can only be that had there been observers, they would have enjoyed such and such impressions. The geologist's land-bridge evaporates into a mere unfulfilled possibility of certain experiences having occurred at a time when nothing existed, for all they tell us, to make them occur.

This was too violent a paradox for even Berkeley to accept, and he took refuge in the following account of the Creation (Dialogue III between Hylas and Philonous) : All possible worlds existed from all eternity in the mind of God. When He created this world He decreed the order in which ideas should be obtainable by finite spirits ; and though we are told that

[1]This objection is developed by Mr. I. Berlin in an article in *mind N.S.*, July, 1950.

He had not yet created man, we are not told that He had not yet created angels.

It would seem then that unless geologists are logically committed to a belief in angels, the phenomenalist solution cannot be accepted. The phenomenalist says that sensations are related to beliefs about material things as observed instences are to inductive generalisations and predictions. The rationalist says they are related as premisses to deductive conclusion. Both are mistaken. The relation in question is of a different and probably peculiar type. Hume's merit is that he saw that this was so, though he failed to give a satisfactory account of the relation.

CHAPTER IX

MINDS
(Treatise Book I, Part IV, Sects. V and VI)

1. *Outline of Hume's view*

THE question of mind, Hume begins by saying, is not "perplexed with any such contradictions as those we have discovered" in our opinions concerning matter. It is "infinitely obscure", but "what is known concerning it agrees with itself; and what is unknown we must be contented to leave so" (p. 221).

This optimistic claim is withdrawn in the Appendix (Treatise, Vol. 2, p. 317). "On a more strict review of the section concerning *personal identity*, I find myself involved in such a labyrinth, that I must confess I neither know how to correct my former opinions, nor how to render them consistent". He sums up his difficulties by saying (p. 319) that there are two principles, neither of which he can give up, but which together make it impossible to account for the unity of consciousness. These principles are that every distinct perception is a distinct existence, and that the mind never discovers any real connexion between distinct existences. I shall discuss these principles later.

Nevertheless Hume could have said that, though his own philosophical system is perplexed with this contradiction concerning the nature of mind, there is no natural and inevitable contradiction in our commonsense convictions concerning the mind, comparable to that which he found in our convictions about matter. Our notion of a permanent and identical self is indeed (according to him) a figment of the imagination, but it is not a figment that is essential to our survival or incorrigible by philosophical reflection.

The mind, Hume says in Section V, is not, as philosophers like the Cartesians maintain, a simple indivisible immaterial (*i.e.*, unextended) substance in which our perceptions inhere. This is the doctrine of "the immateriality of the soul", popular with theologians. Nor, on the other hand, are the materialists correct, who say that the substance in which our perceptions inhere is a material substance or substances, part of the body. Both views have the same fault of being unintelligible. Neither side can say what they mean by "substance" or "inhesion". But some of the arguments used in this senseless dispute are interesting, Hume finds, and suggest interesting conclusions.

In Section VI, "Of Personal Identity", Hume tells us what, as far as he can see, the mind is. It is "nothing but a bundle or collection of different perceptions, which succeed each other with an inconceivable rapidity, and are in a perpetual flux and movement" (p. 239). All the identity that it really possesses is a serial identity, the sort of unity which we find, to take Hume's example, in a "republic or commonwealth" (*i.e.* a political community). In a republic, he explains, the individual citizens are united by various political, legal, and customary relationships, and their descendants, succeeding to these relationships with or without modifying them, continue the existence of that same republic. And as the same republic may not only change its citizens, but also its laws and constitutions, so may the same person "vary his character and disposition, as well as his impressions and ideas, without losing his identity" (p. 247).

In addition to this real serial identity, we indulge in the fiction of something identical in what Hume considers the strict and proper sense of the word, something permanent and unchanging. We do this because we have a natural tendency to confuse a series of related and similar objects with a single unchanging object; for instance, we often call an interrupted series of distinct but similar noises a single noise (p. 244). Similarly, we call the series of different perceptions, interrupted as it is by sleep, a single self. Then, when we are forced to take notice of the interruptions, but still cling to our habit of regarding ourselves as single permanent objects, we get over the conflict by feigning the existence of something distinct from all our perceptions, the "soul" or "self" which has them, and which is supposed to remain one and the same through all its different perceptions, and even when no perceptions are occurring (p. 241).

There is, Hume says, no shadow of empirical evidence for the existence of any such thing. He, at least, cannot find any impression corresponding to this idea, whatever may be the case with "some metaphysicians" (p. 239).

Such in outline are Hume's views, inadequate as he himself confesses them to be on their positive side. Let us consider first in more detail his negative contention that the soul is not a simple indivisible unextended substance in which our perceptions inhere.

2. *The errors of metaphysicians*

On the topic of substance (Part I, Section VI; Part IV, Section V) Hume is brief and positive. Show me, he says, the impression from which the idea of substance is derived. The impressions of sense are all impressions of sensible qualities, colour, shape, sound, taste, smell, etc. None of these is a substance. The impressions of reflection "resolve themselves into our passions and emotions" (p. 24). These are not substances. The substance is supposed to be something which *has* colour, shape, etc., or something which is the subject of the passion or emotion. No such thing can be found.

Hume probably thought that he could afford to be brief in his rejections of the idea of substance in view of what Locke and Berkeley had said of it.

Locke (Essay Concerning the Human Understanding, Book II, ch. 23), attempting to expound the origin of the idea, had exposed it as a confused and relative idea of something *supposed* (not found by experience) as a support of observable qualities; an idea of "something", not in the case of some further-specifiable kind of entity, but just "something, I know not what".

Berkeley, both in the Principles of Human Knowledge, and in the first of the "Three Dialogues of Hylas and Philonous", had shown that this idea of a mere "something" was the mere abstract idea of "quiddity" or "existence" considered apart from any specifiable manner of existence, the most vicious of all vicious abstractions, the bare contradictory of the idea of "nothing".

He had also, in the first dialogue, shown that it could not even claim to be intelligible as a "relative" idea, because no meaning could be assigned to the words, such as "support" and "inherence", used for the relation in which substance was supposed to stand to the perceivable qualities. These terms are plainly metaphorically used, he says, and what they are supposed to indicate cannot be said to resemble in any specifiable way the relations they stand for when used literally. Qualities would not fall to the ground if they had no substance to "support" them.

What was intended by the use of the term "support", was that somehow the qualities could not exist without the substance to exist in. But in what sense could they exist "in" it? Not in the spatial sense of "in", for size, extension itself, is supposed to be one of the qualities requiring a substance to support it; and, as substance would need to have size before anything could be "in" it, it would have to be extended (*i.e.*, support extension) in order to support extension, which leads to a vicious regress.

But Berkeley had directed his attack solely against the idea of corporeal substance. Spiritual substance he thought was not liable to these objections. "Ideas" require a substance to be "in"; that substance must be something that exists. But here we can say what we mean by all these terms; "What is a spirit, show me an instance of it?" "You are one yourself", Berkeley would answer, "you know spirit by being it". "In what sense do I exist?" "You act, will and perceive, your *esse* is *vel percipere vel agere*". "In what sense are my perceptions 'in' me?" "Simply in the sense that you perceive them, and you know what perceiving is, simply by undergoing it". "In what way is my existence necessary to that of my perceptions?" "Their *esse* is *percipi*; there is an odour, it is smelt, there is a colour it is seen, there is a noise, it is heard. The suggestion of unheard sounds, unsmelt smells, etc., is nonsensical".

Hume clearly does not accept Berkeley's account of spiritual substance, though he does not consider Berkeley's views by name, or even seem to have Berkeley principally in mind. We are not, says Hume, aware of ourselves; only of our perceptions. That a perception is perceived, means simply that it is a member of the bundle. A percipient mind is not necessary to the existence of a perception; every perception is a distinct existence in its own right, and nothing is necessary to its existence. If the definition of a substance be "something which may exist by itself", every distinct perception is a substance, and nothing else is (pp. 222–23).

Whether we agree with Hume or with Berkeley, we must, I think, censure Hume for failing to mention and discuss the answers which Berkeley had suggested to the question which Hume asks on p. 222, "What do you mean by substance and inhesion?" Berkeley had offered an interpretation of these words in terms of spirit and perception, an interpretation which can be called "empirical" if we are allowed to include in "experience" that inner awareness of our own activity and passivity of which Berkeley speaks.

We may put the position thus; the terms "substance" and "inhesion", as ordinarily used by metaphysicians, had been shown to be meaningless. Berkeley maintained that they could be given an interpretation in terms of verifiable entities, *sc.* spirits and their ideas, which would make it true that all qualities exist in a substance, a substance being something whose existence does not logically entail the existence of anything else. Hume denied that this was so.

Now it is clear that even if Berkeley is right, the terms "substance" and "inhesion" become quite pointless. The situation described by the sentence "I hear a noise" is familiar; no light at all is thrown on its nature by the suggested alternative expression "The quality of noisiness inheres in a spiritual substance". For "inheres in" now means by definition "is perceived by", and "spiritual substance" means by definition "something like you".

The theologians who supported the doctrine of the immateriality of the soul plainly meant to be more informative when they called the soul a simple substance. They were suggesting a way of thinking of things, a conceptual scheme, from which certain important consequences were supposed to follow.

The sort of view they had in mind may be put as follows: all natural changes consist in rearrangements of existing things; nothing new is created and nothing is destroyed by natural changes. Therefore, natural change can only bring into existence or destroy composite things. But if there are composite things, there must be simple things of which they are made, and these will be uncreatable and indestructible by natural causes. These simple things are of two kinds: material atoms, and spiritual atoms, or individual souls; each human being consists of an individual soul animating a composite material body. This soul is therefore a separate individual entity, neither created by the natural process of birth nor destroyed by the natural process of death, or any other natural process.

This conception of the soul, compatible both with the Christian theological system and with the transmigratory systems of the Pythagoreans and certain oriental religions, found its way into Christian thought through the Greek philosophers. It is radically opposed to any Pantheistic doctrine, such as that of Spinoza, according to whom the soul was not a separate individual substance, but a mere attribute or mode of God, the one and only underlying substance of all things, both mental and material. That is why Hume takes such malicious delight in elaborating his complicated *argumentum ad hominem*, to show that the doctrine of the immateriality of the soul really amounts to the same thing as the doctrine of Spinoza (p. 228 ff.).

Now, whatever truth we may recognise in Berkeley's claim that we are aware of ourselves as percipient and active entities, it is quite certain that we are not aware of ourselves by any sort of inner consciousness as simple indivisible indestructible substances.[1] We can, therefore, consider separately the objections which Hume makes to the doctrine of the simple indivisible substantial soul, and those he makes against the claim that we are aware of ourselves as percipient active entities.

Hume's main objection to the theologians is, as we have seen, that the notions of substance and inhesion are unintelligible. The whole question, in what sort of substance do thoughts inhere, is nonsensical. But he cannot forbear to point

---

[1] Though Berkeley does say that a spirit is a simple indivisible incorporeal thing, I do not know on what grounds he thought so, or see that any important consequences follow from its simplicity, once the analogy with material atoms has been abandoned.

out that some of the principal arguments used by the theologians and the materialists are nonsensical in another respect as well.

The materialists argue that our perceptions of touch and sight, for instance our perceptions of a table, are extended (p. 228). They have shape and size ; indeed, such perceptions are the foundation of our notions of shape and size. How can an extended perception inhere in an unextended substance, as the theologians pretend ?

The theologians retort that many of our perceptions are unextended, and the ideas of shape, size and position are simply inapplicable to them. "Can anyone conceive a passion a yard in length, a foot in breadth, and an inch in thickness ?" (p. 224). And is it not absurd to suppose "that several passions may be placed in a circular figure, and that a certain number of smells conjoined with a certain number of sounds, may make a body of twelve cubic inches ?" (p. 227). How, the theologians ask, can such unextended perceptions inhere in an extended substance ? How, that is, can thoughts be in the brain, or any other part of the body ? If the perception inheres in the whole body, it has the shape of the whole ; if it inheres only in a part it will have the shape and position of the part, and passions, for instance, will have positions relative to one another, will be below, above, to the left of, to the right of one another, which is absurd.

Consideration of these arguments leads Hume to ask the question, what objects can have size, shape, and position in space ? (p. 224). He answers, only perceptions of sight and touch, from which our "first notion of space and extension is derived solely". Nothing but what is visible or tangible has parts so disposed as to convey the idea of space. Smells, tastes, noises do not, properly speaking, have shape, size or position.

It is true, he admits, that we think of the taste of a fig as "in the fig", and of the taste of an olive as "in the olive". But first, suppose the fig to be at one end of the table and the olive at the other, say 8 feet apart, does it really make sense to say that the two tastes are 8 feet apart ? Secondly, is the taste of the fig in a certain part of the fig ? No, the whole fig tastes of fig. Is it then in the whole fig ? In that case the taste must have the shape and size of the fig, which is absurd.

What happens, says Hume, is that, finding the fig to be the cause of the taste and their ideas closely associated in the imagination, we tend to cement the alliance, as it were, by bestowing on them other relations, among which is conjunction in space, although, strictly speaking, the taste cannot be said to have position in space at all (p. 226). Then finding that we cannot clearly conceive the spatial conjunction of the two (is it in the whole fig or a part of it, etc. ?), we fall into a hopelessly confused way of thinking, and regard the taste as existing entire in the whole fig and entire in every part of it, as the scholastics used to say, "*totum in toto, et totum in qualibet parte*" (p. 227).

Hume concludes, that of many things, it is true to say that they exist, but exist nowhere (p. 224).

If this is so, the arguments of both theologians and materialists fall to the ground. The question "how do unextended perceptions exist in the extended brain ?" is not more difficult than the question "how does the taste exist in the fig ?" Strictly speaking the perceptions are nowhere, and therefore not in the brain at all ; loosely speaking they are *in* the brain in the sense that they are caused by and associated in our minds with the brain, just as the taste is similarly related to the fig.

The question "how can extended perceptions be *in* an unextended soul ?" is equally pointless. Strictly speaking the unextended soul (if there could be such a thing) would be nowhere, and incapable of containing or being otherwise spatially related to anything. Loosely speaking the extended perception could be "contained in" or "part of" the soul, in the same sense as a move in a game of chess is "part of" a plan, or "contained in" it. The move occurs on the board, the plan is nowhere; but they are so related that such talk is customary and significant.

Before leaving Hume's section "On the Immateriality of the Soul" we must consider one other interesting passage, in which he discusses the action of body on mind (p. 234).

He first sets out in forcible terms an argument whose " seeming evidence" "few have been able to withstand": bodies, however divided, conjoined, or moved, remain bodies; no conceivable movements or impacts of bodies constitute a thought, which is something of a totally different kind; and as these "shocks, variations and mixtures are the only changes of which matter is susceptible . . . it is concluded to be impossible that thought can ever be caused by matter".

Starting from his own view of causation, Hume makes short work of this argument. It is simply a complaint that there is no discoverable connexion between any movement of matter and the occurrence of a thought. But there is no discoverable connexion says Hume, between any cause and its effect; for instance there is no discoverable connexion between the relative positions and sizes of the earth and the sun and the resulting movement in accordance with the laws of gravity. Size and distance are just size and distance, and the idea of motion cannot be extracted from them, any more than the idea of thought can.

Hume reduces his argument to a dilemma. Either you say there can be no causal relation where there is no discoverable connexion, in which case you end up by denying all causation; or you admit causation wherever there is constant conjunction, in which case you must admit that our perceptions are often due to material causes. We must, he says, separate the question of the union of soul and body and the substance of the soul, from that concerning the cause of its thought; "confining ourselves to the latter question, we find, by comparing their ideas, that thought and motion are different from each other, and by experience that they are constantly united".

It seems to me impossible to improve on this terse and lucid statement of the position. But it is possible to suggest certain better reasons which philosophers and scientists have for being dissatisfied with any account of the interaction of mind and body they can give; better reasons, that is, than the argument which Hume refutes.

There is a perfectly good sense in which it is true to say that we cannot explain *how*, for instance, certain physical changes in the brain cause a sensation of yellow, although it is an indubitable fact that they do. It is true in the sense that we cannot derive this special correlation from any general law of nature. That specific change in the brain might have been constantly conjoined with the sensation of red instead of yellow, without any law of physics or psychology, or any other systematic science, being broken ; equally it might have been

K

constantly conjoined with a tactual sensation or with no sensation at all. Science can offer no "theoretical explanation" of psycho-physical correlations.

3. *Self-consciousness and personal identity*

We must now turn to Hume's section "Of Personal Identity".

I shall suggest first that the self is not, as Hume says, "nothing but a bundle or collection of different perceptions"; and that even if it were what he intends to convey by that phrase and the sentence in which it occurs (p. 239), it could possess "identity" in a perfectly proper and usual sense of the term, without any fiction of the imagination being required.

Secondly, I shall suggest that there are certain important mistakes in the reasoning which lead him to adopt this view, mistakes which land him in the embarrassment he complains of in the Appendix to Vol. 2 of the Treatise.

If we look at the opening paragraphs of the section we see that it is not philosophers such as Descartes or the metaphysical theologians, considered in his section "On the Immateriality of the Soul", that Hume is now opposing. It is philosophers who believe in the existence of self on *empirical* grounds, who claim to feel its existence, its continuance and its perfect identity and simplicity (p. 238).

In the first two paragraphs Hume offers five arguments against the existence of the self.

(I) We have no impression of self.

(II) We could not have such an impression; the suggestion is self-contradictory.

(III) If the self is permanent and identical, the impression from which it is derived must abide without interruption or alteration throughout our lives. No impression does this.

(IV) All my perceptions are distinct and separable existencies, and require nothing to support their existence. How then can they belong to a self, how can they be connected with it?

(V) The occurrence of my particular perceptions is all that is necessary for, and is sufficient for my existence. So long as they occur, I am; when they cease, I am not. Therefore I am they.

I suggest that arguments (I) and (II) rest on the same mistake. The trouble is in the word "impression". As we saw when considering Part I of the Treatise, "impression", partly owing to the history of the word, inevitably suggested "sensation" (whether external or internal) and "idea" inevitably suggested "image". Now it is certainly true that the self is not known to us in a sensation of any sort, in the same way as a colour, a sound, or an emotion is. Equally certainly we can form no image of the self. But, as we saw, when Hume asserts that all our ideas are derived from impressions, the principle he has in mind is not really one about sensations and images. It is the principle that we can think about nothing but what is given us in experience to think about.

I suggest that there is much plausibility in Berkeley's view, that we have an experience which we call the self or soul, an experience different in kind from our other experiences, more internal than the most personal emotion we feel, and not needing or able to be represented in thought by an image, since in all thinking it is actually present. For these reasons he calls it a "notion" and not an "idea". If we accept this suggestion, the contradiction complained of in Hume's argument (II) vanishes. It would be, indeed, a contradiction to have an impression of that which is no impression but "to which all our impressions have a reference". But it is not self-contradictory to suppose that that which has all other experiences has also a special inner experience of its own existence.

Argument (III) rests on a mistake about the proper meaning of the terms "identity", "the same". According to Hume our idea of identity is the idea of something that continues without interruption and without change; when we attribute identity to changing objects such as plants, animals and machines, we speak loosely and support our inaccurate use of words by a fiction of the imagination, a fiction of some unobservable unchanging thing. I suggest that the fundamental idea of identity is simply that of the unity of an aggregate. How the members of the aggregate must be related to one another in order to form *one* aggregate depends on the sort of aggregate in question. The members of Parliament form one Parliament, but several parties.

A common kind of identity is that of the unity of a series. It remains one series so long as each member is related to its predecessors in a certain characteristic way. The series of whole numbers is one series because each member is greater by one than the preceding member. There is thus no reason why the self should not change, and even suffer interruptions in its existence, and yet preserve its identity; just as a play is the same play despite the interval between the acts and the change of scene. And a play is one of the things to which Hume compares the mind (pp. 239–40). We do not feign any metaphysical entity when we think of a play as being the same play resumed after an interval, or with a change of actors and scenery. It is the substantiality of the self, not its identity, which requires a fiction, if anything does.

The fourth and fifth arguments are the most interesting and the most difficult to understand. Argument (IV) (p. 239), appears to say that since our "particular perceptions" are different, distinguishable, separable from each other, capable of being considered separately, and have no need of anything to support their existence, they cannot belong to a self or be connected with it. This is a curious argument, and it is difficult to see just what does follow from the welter of premises offered to us.

As far as I can see, the premises are really two in number.

(a) Every perception is logically independent of every other perception; *i.e.*, it involves no contradiction to suppose of any given perception that it occurred, but that the other perceptions that preceded, accompanied and followed it were other than they in fact were, or even that no other perceptions preceded, accompanied or followed it. This is the central thesis of Hume's denial of objective necessary connexion.

(b) Every perception is logically independent of the existence of any other entity whatsoever. The occurrence of a perception does not logically entail the existence of any other thing, *e.g.*, a mind to which it belongs, or an external substance that causes it.

Now I cannot see that the non-existence of the self follows from either or both of these premises, even if they are true.

I shall discuss later whether they are true or not. Even if it is not logically necessary that every perception should belong to a connected whole of experience or to a self, yet some perceptions may, in fact, be related to one another in a certain peculiar way, and also related to a self; and it does seem to be an empirical fact that when I am aware of two perceptions, say a loud noise and a feeling of fear, and compare them or consider them together, as Hume constantly speaks of himself as doing, there is a relation between these two perceptions which does not exist between a loud noise heard by me and a feeling of fear felt by you. The former pair are what psychologists call "co-presented"; they are united in one consciousness, whatever that may mean. In short, the argument is a *non sequitur*, and the conclusion is false as a matter of empirical fact.

Yet it was just this argument that caused Hume such trouble in the Appendix to the Treatise. If perceptions are distinct existences, and the mind never perceives a connexion between distinct existences, how, he asks, do they become united in a single consciousness, as they plainly do?

Now the connexion which Hume maintains we never find between distinct existences is logically necessary connexion. But this is plainly not the sort of connexion we require to explain the unity of consciousness. For no one supposes that all the perceptions of a single mind are logically connected like the axioms and theorems of a geometrical system; there is, for instance, no logical connexion between having a headache on Tuesday and hearing a cuckoo on Thursday. The only question is what relation does in fact unite perceptions in one consciousness?

Hume rightly sees that it cannot be similarity, causation, or local or temporal conjunction. All these relations, except local conjunction, of which only some perceptions are susceptible, may hold between the perceptions of different minds as much as between the perceptions of a single mind[1]; and these relations Hume assumed, for no good reason, to be the only alternatives.

They are, I suggest, not the only alternatives; there is an

[1] I assume here that telepathy does in fact occur.

empirically given relation which we may call co-presentation,
which holds between any two or more perceptions which I am
in a position to compare with one another; and it looks very
much as if it were an empirical fact that this relation is at
least a three-term relation, involving at least two perceptions
and something else, the mind to which they are presented and
which is able to compare them. I say only that it looks as if there
were this third term, because the admission of it is liable to
a difficulty which is closely connected with Hume's fifth
argument.

In argument (V) Hume says first, that he can never at any
time catch himself without a perception; a mind without a
perception does not, as a matter of observable fact, ever occur;
and secondly, that as a matter of logic a mind without a perception is inconceivable. The cessation of all my perceptions
would be as complete an annihilation of myself as I can
imagine.

Both these propositions seem to me to be true; and if the
second is true, then the third term I spoke of above is a very
curious kind of entity. It is not a perception, but the existence
of perceptions is logically necessary to its existence. I am so
persuaded of the fundamental truth of Hume's distinction
between logical connexions and factual conjunctions, that
I cannot, on reflexion admit the existence of such an entity.

If the self is something distinct from its perceptions, as a
house is distinct from its occupants, then the perceptions
cannot be logically necessary to the existence of the self, any
more than the occupants can be logically necessary to the
existence of the house. If, on the other hand, perceptions are
logically necessary to the existence of the self, as citizens are
logically necessary to the existence of a state, then the self is
no more an entity distinct from its perceptions than the state
is an entity distinct from its citizens; it is rather a form of
relational pattern in which they are combined.

The conclusion to which we are driven is that the self is
not an entity distinct from its perceptions, but consists of
perceptions suitably related. The relations required to unite
them are not merely similarity, causation and spatial and
temporal conjunction, but also co-presentation. Hume failed
to recognise the existence of this relation as an empirical fact,

and therefore found himself in the difficulty described in the Appendix to the Treatise.

I have now completed my case for two of my suggestions. First, the self is not a mere bundle of perceptions; it is at least a very peculiar form of relational unity of perceptions. Secondly, Hume's arguments rested on three mistakes: (a) the mistake about the proper meaning of the term identity; (b) his too narrow view of what could be the origin of an idea, due to the misleading implications of the term "impression"; (c) the mistake of supposing that logically necessary connexion was the only relation which could unite our perceptions in a single consciousness.

It remains to make a case for my third suggestion that even if the self were merely a bundle or collection of perceptions related only by the relations of resemblance, causation, succession and simultaneity, it could yet have an identity in a natural and proper sense of that word (although, of course, it would lack the peculiar sort of unity which it in fact has). This follows from what I have said about the meaning of "identity". A Humean self could well have exactly the same sort of serial identity which a play or a republic has; as long as each of its perceptions was related to those that went before in the right sort of way it would remain the same self.

Not only is this a possible sense of "personal identity", it is a sense in which the expression actually tends to be used. In cases where they find a sharp causal and qualitative discontinuity in the thoughts, emotions, desires and actions associated with a given body, psychologists say there are two persons, or personalities, present, or that the personality is divided. And they do this even in cases where the relation of co-presentation still holds between perceptions in one of the personalities and perceptions in the other.

Nevertheless, on reconsidering all that I have said, I feel perplexed and dissatisfied, as Hume did when he wrote the Appendix. If the self is only a relational unity of perceptions, connected by co-presentation and other empirical relations, that inner awareness of our own being, of which Berkeley speaks, remains unaccounted for; and anyway the relation of co-presentation remains somewhat mysterious.

The difficulty has been formulated by someone in a hexa-

metrical criticism of Hume, "How can a series of conscious
states be aware of itself as a series?" But when I consider this
hexameter, I see that the difficulty is wrongly put. It is not the
series as a whole which is required to be aware of itself. We
are not self-conscious all the time. We are self-conscious at
certain times. It is some of the members of the series that must
be aware of themselves as members of the series. Just as when
a nation is said to be conscious of its own existence as a nation,
it is really the members of the nation, or some of them, who
are aware of themselves as members of the nation.

But still, what is it for a perception to be aware of itself as
a member of that relational unity of perceptions we call a
mind? I do not know the answer to this question.

PART II

HUME'S ACCOUNT OF MORALITY

CHAPTER I

INTRODUCTORY

HUME'S moral philosophy has met with much disfavour among later moralists. It has been complained that he does less than justice to the part played by reason in moral judgements and in moral conduct; that the "moral sentiment" on which he bases his theory is just one human feeling on a level with the others, and that it fails to account for that superior authority and urgency which are characteristic of what we call "conscience"; that in saying that the moral sentiment is actuated always, however indirectly, by considerations of pleasure and pain, he ranks himself with the hedonists, whose outlook is fundamentally base and unworthy of the dignity of man, as well as untrue to the facts; and finally that by founding morality on feeling he makes it a relative and subjective matter, and forfeits all hopes of a universally valid and objective system of morals.

And yet, if we state the essence of Hume's theory shortly and in common language, what is it? Simply this: first, that by calling an action virtuous or vicious, we mean simply that when we consider it generally and without reference to our own personal interests we have a feeling of approval or disapproval for it, approval being a feeling of joy and pleasure, disapproval one of uneasiness, pain or disgust; and secondly, that what makes us approve or disapprove actions when so considered is simply their tendency to promote the happiness or unhappiness (*i.e.*, pleasure or pain) of those, whoever they may be, who are affected by the actions in question, directly or indirectly.

Whatever may be the reactions of moralists of the more elevated type, I venture to assert that this account cannot but recommend itself at first view to commonsense.

It may be feared, of course, that this account offers too
little inducement to be virtuous, and compares in this respect
unfavourably with other views.

If I tell a youth that he is a composite being, containing,
beside the natural or animal part of his make-up, a divine
part, which is reason, and that morality consists in adhering
to the immutable laws of reason; or, alternatively, if I tell him
that the divine part is love, and that morality consists in the
exercise of love, which may be fanned through the offices of
religion by the breath of God; if I tell him something like this,
I indeed give him a powerful incentive to virtue. But the
incentive depends on his believing the factual propositions
I assert. And it does not appear that the religious convictions
of men are more stable than their moral characters.

Similarly, if I tell a youth that morality is simply interest
on the long view; that honesty does not merely happen as
a matter of fact to be the best policy, but is simply the name
of what is, in the long run, for economic or theological reasons,
the agent's own best interest in this world or the next; in this
case I again provide a powerful incentive to virtue. But again
its power depends on his believing certain propositions, which
he may well come, as a result of experience or other causes,
to doubt.

Perhaps it is a safer method to point out just what, as
a matter of observable fact, happens in us when we pass moral
judgements on the conduct of ourselves and others, and when
we feel shame or satisfaction with our own past behaviour, or
scruples and obligations with regard to our future behaviour.
Perhaps it is safer to describe the nature, causes, and effects of
the moral sentiment, as observation shows them to be, and
leave it to each individual, so instructed, to choose whether he
shall attach more importance to it than to other sentiments.
Let him accept morality, if he accepts it, for what it can be
ascertained to be; and leave speculations about its supernatural
or other origins to be treated as a separate question.

But, at this point, it will be objected that Hume equally
asks us to believe certain rather sweeping factual statements,
which many will doubt; and as long as they are doubted his
philosophy is not much help in clarifying the nature of the
choice between virtue and vice; the only difference is that

these propositions are psychological propositions, not propositions of theology or economics ; and psychology is a highly controversial subject.

Now, if we look again at the brief outline I have given of the essence of Hume's theory of morals, we can see that it may be restated in a way that omits the psychological propositions.

By calling an action virtuous or vicious we mean that when we consider it generally and without reference to our own personal interests, we approve or disapprove of it, and that what makes us approve or disapprove of it, when so considered, is simply its tendency to promote the happiness or unhappiness of all who may be in any way affected by it.

In this restatement we have left out the assertion that approval and disapproval are feelings, respectively pleasant and unpleasant, and that happiness and unhappiness consist in pleasure and pain. It is assumed that we know what approval and disapproval, happiness and unhappiness are when we meet them in ourselves and others; and it is asserted that the approval and disapproval which we call "moral" are generalised and impersonal attitudes excited by considerations of utility and disutility, production of happiness and unhappiness.

It would appear then that the essence of Hume's theory, purged of its psychological element, consists in a plausible and wholesome philosophical contention; that there is a connexion between the meanings of the terms "moral", "approval" and "disapproval", "happiness" and "unhappiness", which makes it nonsense to say that an action is morally right or wrong, but does not command your disinterested approval or disapproval on grounds of its tendency to promote the happiness or unhappiness of those affected by it.

It must be confessed, indeed, that Hume often, particularly in the Treatise, fails to distinguish the philosophical and psychological elements in his theory, and therefore uses a great many psychological arguments to support philosophical propositions. His psychological accounts of the nature and causes of approval and disapproval, happiness and unhappiness are defective; and on the philosophical side, as we shall see, his analysis of "reason" is unduly narrow. These defects lend some colour to the objections mentioned in the first paragraph of this chapter. But even taken with these defects his theory, considered as a theory, is extremely coherent and ingenious.

When we turn to the Enquiry we find not only a simpler and less dubious psychology, but also the most convincing praises of virtue. The godless Epicurean of the eighteenth century was not less eloquent on this topic than his prototypes of antiquity. Like them he believed that God is not terrible, that the dead feel nothing and that happiness is attainable by human intelligence and virtue. Like them he put his convictions into practice in his life and in his death, though fortunately the illness that killed him was less painful than the gallstones of which Epicurus died.

CHAPTER II

THE SERVITUDE OF REASON

1. *Reason alone never influences action* (Treatise Book II, Part III, Sect. III; Enquiry Sect. I, and Appendix I).

HUME has seldom caused more scandal to philosophers than when he said that "Reason is, and ought only to be, the slave of the passions, and can never pretend to any other office than to serve and obey them" (p. 127), and that, as a consequence of this, as well as on other grounds, "it is in vain to pretend that morality is discovered only by a deduction of reason" (p. 167).

Had not Socrates said that virtue was knowledge, Plato defined justice as a harmony of the passions and desires under the direction of reason, and Aristotle, though he had admitted that "the understanding itself moves nothing", added that there was something called "the practical understanding", consisting in the direction of desire to that which reason pronounced good, and capable of causing action?

The Stoics had identified virtue and happiness with conformity to reason, and a long line of Christian thinkers had believed in "Natural Law" (in the moral sense of "law"), which they conceived to be in essence rational and intelligible to human reason, and to comprise the fundamental principles of justice. Of this last-named school, Hooker and Locke were eminent and fairly recent examples in Hume's time.

The scandal would have been less had Hume maintained that the non-rational source of moral distinctions was in any way supernatural; that it consisted, for instance, in conscience, conceived, as Bishop Butler conceived it, as an intimation from God of where our true obligations and our true happiness lay; or that it was the motive of Christian Charity, conceived as a motive superior to all others because it was one that man

159

shared with God, and possessed only by the inspiration of the Spirit of God.

But Hume said that, on the contrary, the foundation of moral distinctions was a moral sentiment, which was perfectly natural in origin, arose as the result of discoverable psychological processes, and was actuated in part by objects (institutions of property and contract) which were of man's own contrivance.

I may add that I find that these contentions of Hume still scandalise many of my pupils.

The first argument which Hume uses is that moral judgements do influence our actions; sometimes, however rarely, men do things because it is their duty to do them, and in opposition to their desires. But, Hume says, reason cannot cause or prevent any action, or oppose any passion or desire. Therefore reason cannot be the source of moral judgements.

Let us examine Hume's case for the practical impotence of reason, given in Book II, Part III, Sect. III.

We must first note that Hume expressly confines the term " reason " to the two branches of the understanding which he has studied in Book I of the Treatise, *viz.*, the tracing of abstract relations of ideas (demonstrative reasoning) and causal inferences to matters of fact (reasoning from experience). To apply the term reason to anything else is, he says, to speak improperly, although we do often speak thus improperly of something very important, as we shall see later.

Hume first deals briskly and briefly with demonstrative reasoning; he thinks "it scarce will be asserted" that this species of reasoning "alone is ever the cause of any action. As its proper province is the world of ideas, and as the will always places us in that of realities, demonstration and volition seem upon that account to be totally removed from one another". He then admits that mathematics, the principal field of demonstrative reasoning, has a use in practical affairs, "in almost every art and profession". But this he says is only because it serves to "direct our judgement concerning causes and effects".

There seem to be two distinct arguments here, which we must sort out and state distinctly.

First, when Hume says that the proper province of demonstration is the world of ideas, whereas the will is concerned with realities, I take it he is repeating his valid contention that no matter of fact can be demonstrated *a priori*. As Descartes had observed, the demonstrations of mathematicians prove only hypothetical propositions; *e.g.*, "If any object is triangular, its internal angles will be equal to two right angles". Only experience can tell us that a certain object is triangular. From this it follows that, since action is always concerned with actual objects, experience as well as deductive reasoning is necessary to produce action. Calculations and deductions cannot help us without data derived from experience. So far so good. No rationalistic moralist would attempt to deny this.

Secondly, Hume asserts that even if experience provides us with the data—say the sums of money I have paid to a certain person, and the goods, with their prices, which I have received from him—the calculation which demonstrates the difference between the two in terms of money is only of practical interest because of the causes and effects of that difference; *e.g.*, the fact that if I do not pay him a sum equal to the difference he will sue me at law and provide me with no more goods.

This second contention of Hume's will seem to some to be dubious. It might well be asked, is it not precisely the fact that the goods received were worth £10 more than I have paid which imposes on me the obligation to pay him £10? Or rather, is not this difference just what we mean by a debt of £10, and is not the knowledge of this debt just what causes me, if I am honest, to pay the man £10?

Hume would reply first, that even if we allow that my calculations reveal a peculiar quality in the situation, *viz.*, my indebtedness, the effect of this discovery on my actions will depend on another and variable factor. The discovery may lead me to pay the debt, or it may lead me to leave the country or otherwise evade my creditors ; it would depend, according to Hume, on how I *felt* about this quality, *i.e.*, on its effects on me. And second, that the indebtedness itself, as discovered by the calculations, is not a moral fact at all. The calculations only reveal a certain numerical proportion between the values of the goods received and the sums of money paid; they conclude in a proposition of the form x–y = £10. There is no inference possible from this to the moral proposition "I ought to pay so and so £10".

It is, indeed, possible to use the term "debt" to describe a situation such as the calculations reveal; in that case, "I am in debt" only means "I have received more than I have paid". It does not mean "I ought to pay the difference", any more than it means "Well done me; I must hang on to my profit". The moral proposition "Debts ought to be paid" is still to seek.

It is also possible to use the term "debt" to mean "a sum of money which ought to be paid over". In that case the moral proposition "debts ought to be paid" is a tautology. But the proposition "I am in debt" is no longer the conclusion of my calculations.

The point at issue here is made by Hume in a celebrated passage (Treatise, Book III, Part I, Sect. I, p. 177).

> "In every system of morality which I have hitherto met with, I have always remarked, that the author proceeds for some time in the ordinary way of reasoning, and establishes the being of a God, or makes some observations concerning human affairs; when of a sudden I am surprised to find that instead of the usual copulation of propositions, *is*, and *is not*, I meet with no proposition that is not connected with an *ought*, or an *ought not*. This change is imperceptible; but is, however, of the last consequence. For as this *ought*, or *ought not*, expresses some new relation or affirmation, it is necessary that it should be observed and explained; and at the same time, that a reason should be given, for what seems altogether inconceivable, how this new relation can be a deduction from others, which are entirely different from it".

We may state Hume's general position thus: experience tells us what is, and by inductive inference what probably will be, would be, or would have been; demonstrative reasoning traces the connexions between the ideas by which we represent in our thought what is or what might be. These are the only forms of reasoning we have. But "ought" and "ought not" do not stand for any such actual or possible existences, nor yet for ways of representing them in our thought. They, therefore, do not stand for anything discoverable by reason.

We have now largely anticipated Hume's argument to

prove that empirical reasoning concerning matters of fact cannot by itself move us to action.

This reasoning he says only discovers the causes and effects of observed or remembered objects. And these discoveries only move us to action if the causes and effects discovered excite desire or aversion. This they can only do if they hold out a prospect of pleasure or pain. It is, therefore, not the reasoning alone, but the desires and aversions excited by its conclusions which move us to action. "It can never in the least concern us to know that such objects are causes and such others effects, if both the causes and effects be indifferent to us".

We may note that "the prospect of pain or pleasure" is not so important a link in this argument as Hume supposes. The real point is that neither the rational expectation of pleasure and pain, or of any other object, can excite us to action, unless we feel desire or aversion for it. And the step from expecting something to desiring or fearing it is not an inference of reason.

2. *The indirect influence of reason on action* (Treatise Book II, Part III, Sect. III)

Hume is, however, far from denying that feelings and actions can be in *any sense* reasonable or unreasonable. A passion, or the action which it produces, can be called reasonable or unreasonable, "so far as it is accompanied with some judgement or opinion" (p. 127). This accompanying judgement may indirectly influence the action in two ways, he says, either by discovering the existence of an object which arouses a passion, or by discovering the causes of some state of affairs which we desire, and so showing us how it can be brought about.[1]

Thus it is unreasonable to pursue an object, if the evidence goes to show that it does not exist; and it is unreasonable to pursue an object by means which experience shows to be unlikely to bring it about; but, he says, "where a passion is neither founded on false suppositions, nor chooses means insufficient for the end, the understanding can neither justify it nor condemn it. It is not contrary to reason to prefer the

[1] In the Enquiry (Sect. I, para. 137) Hume seems to allow that moral decisions may be influenced by reason in more varied and complicated ways. "In order to pave the way for such a sentiment, and give a proper discernment of its object, it is often necessary . . . that . . . nice distinctions be made, just conclusions drawn, distant comparisons formed, complicated relations examined and general facts fixed and ascertained".

destruction of the whole world to the scratching of my finger. It is not contrary to reason for me to choose my total ruin, to prevent the least uneasiness of an Indian, or person wholly unknown to me" (p. 128).

Hume's wording in these passages is, possibly by design, such as to cover two distinct kinds of unreasonable action, which, however, he does not explicitly distinguish.

In the first kind, the accompanying judgement or opinion is itself reasonable, but the passion or action is not influenced by it. For instance, my reason may tell me that a certain pastime I very much enjoyed in youth will no longer give me the same pleasure in middle age, but I may continue to desire that pleasure and pursue it. More frequently, it is some combination of passions that are not influenced by the sound judgements of reason; as when I "will the end but not the means". For instance, I wish to perform all my duties efficiently and know that I cannot do so unless I relinquish some of my numerous offices, but I am unwilling to relinquish any of them.

In the second kind the accompanying judgement is itself unreasonable, though the passions and action may be influenced by it. For instance, wishing to ascertain my speed in the dark, I stop my car under a street-lamp in order to read my speedometer. This is the type of case Hume principally seems to have in mind; and it is the former type which Hume is often accused, with some justification, of neglecting. But he could still say that in both cases all that reason does is to make the factual judgement. The passions and actions are either influenced by the judgement in the ways he describes, or they are not influenced at all.

Hume later makes the point, which applies only to the second kind of unreasonable behaviour, that mistakes of fact "so far from being the source of all immorality . . . are commonly very innocent, and draw no manner of guilt upon the person who is so unfortunate as to fall into them" (Book III, Part III, Sect. I, p. 169).

He could also have made the point that in the first kind of unreasonable action, the failure of the reasonable judgement to modify the action does not of itself make the action wrong. It depends on what sort of an action it is. It is foolish, but not morally wrong to continue to seek pleasure where I know I will

not find it. It is wrong as well as foolish to cling to more offices
than I can efficiently discharge.

The common ground of these two points is well brought
out by Hume in another passage on p. 169: "As the very
essence of morality is supposed (*sc.* by the rationalists) to
consist in an agreement or disagreement to reason, the other
circumstances are entirely arbitrary, and can never bestow on
any action the character of virtuous or vicious, or deprive it of
that character". In short, the rationalist cannot account for the
difference between foolish and morally bad behaviour.

3. *The influence of "Reason" improperly so-called* (Treatise Book II, Part III, Sect. III)

There is another sense in which passions and actions can
be called reasonable or unreasonable, which involves, Hume
thinks, a definite misuse of the term "reason", not merely an
indirect reference to it.

There are, he says, certain "calm", but often "strong",
passions in us, the operation of which feels very like that of
reason. These passions have very general objects, are relatively
permanent through life, and act without producing any sensible
disturbance in the soul. They are, therefore, confused with
reason, and when they oppose the more violent and transitory
passions, we say that "reason" is curbing passion and controlling our actions.

As instances of these calm passions he gives "benevolence
and resentment, the love of life, and kindness to children; or
the general appetite to good and aversion to evil, considered
merely as such" (p. 129). By good and evil he here means
pleasure and pain, as is plain from the opening paragraph of
Book II, Part III, Sect. IX "Of the direct passions".

Now we may agree with Hume that in most cases the
operation of such passions is improperly called "reason", and
that there is a tendency to use the word in this sense. But there
is a special way in which the calm passions operate, of which
Hume has much to say later, in the description of which the
term "reason" seems much less improper. At present I shall
only notice it briefly in anticipation, and refer to a passage
(Book III, Part III, Sect. I, p. 279), where he describes the
way in which the partiality of our moral judgements is checked,

and considerations of convenience lead us to adopt a general impartial standpoint, and to regulate our sentiments by general rules.

It is natural, he says, that our feelings of approval and disapproval should be stronger in proportion as we are nearer in place and time to the action, or personally interested in it, or personally attached to the persons affected by it. But we find that, since these personal factors are constantly changing, and are frequently contrary to those of other people with whom we wish to converse or deal, a most disagreeable and inconvenient confusion and contradiction arises if we adhere to such partial judgements; this discovery calls into play the calm passion of the dislike of evil, *i.e.*, discomfort, as such.

Seeking for an alternative standard of judgement, we find that another calm, regular and general passion provides one, that is sympathy, or the general liking for human happiness— and, indeed, animal happiness—as such. Consequently, to a certain extent we adopt a general point of view in our moral judgements, and annex the terms "right" and "wrong", etc., to conduct beneficial to whoever may be affected by it, whether near or remote from ourselves, known or unknown, friendly or unfriendly to us.

Now it seems to me that this tendency to judge impartially and in accordance with general rules, this tendency to avoid contradiction, disagreement and confusion, this aversion to the arbitrary, the personal and the subjective, is something which it is not improper to call "reason". It is very like what Kant called practical reason, the subordination of our maxims to universal laws; and it is also like that correction by "general rules," which Hume had himself allowed to play a large part in those inferences with regard to matters of fact, which he now speaks of as one of the provinces of "reason" in the proper sense.

If it be once granted that this is a proper use of the term "reason", then there is a form of reasoning with regard to which Hume's objections to the influence of reason on conduct and moral judgement are not intended to apply. Reason, in this sense, is not concerned with truth and falsehood, probability and improbability, except incidentally. It is concerned with order and confusion, harmony and conflict, constancy ·and inconstancy.

Passions and actions, as Hume rightly observes (p. 167) are not the sort of things to which such terms as "truth" and "falsehood", etc., are applicable ; such terms are applicable only to propositions and beliefs. But they are the sort of things to which such terms as "order" and "confusion", "harmony" and "conflict", "constancy" and "inconstancy" apply, as Hume himself admits. Reason, in this sense, is not something distinct from passion and desire, it is simply a kind of ordering of the passions and desires under the prevalence of certain of those that are calm and general. There is, therefore, no difficulty in seeing how it can influence conduct. And Hume admits that it does to a certain extent influence conduct.

Finally, reason, in this sense, does, according to Hume, include the regulation by general rules of those sentiments which the terms "ought" and "ought not" serve to express. Indeed, he says, the proper use of moral terms is to express those sentiments when so regulated; therefore reason, in this sense, is directly concerned with the making of valid moral judgements.

We must, therefore, ask ourselves carefully, before quarrelling with Hume's doctrine of the servitude of reason, whether we differ from him in believing that demonstrative or inductive reasoning is the source of moral judgements and can be a cause of action, in which case our difference will be one of substance and fact, or whether we disagree with him only on a terminological question, because we think that the regulation of sentiments by general rules in the interests of harmony and constancy is part of what is normally and properly meant by the term "reason".

4. *Challenge to Rationalists* (Treatise Book III, Part I, Sect. I; Enquiry, Appendix I)

Hume issues a challenge first to those who maintain that "there are eternal fitnesses and unfitnesses of things" which are discoverable by demonstration and impose an obligation on all rational beings, including the Deity; "show me", says Hume, "what these relations of fitness and unfitness are" (pp. 166, 167, 173); and secondly, to those who assert that virtue and vice consist in some empirical features which can be observed or inferred in certain actions, *e.g.*, wilful murder; "show me what these features are" (p. 177).

The first challenge, actually addressed to such philosophers as Locke, Price and Clarke, but chiefly noteworthy for the valiant attempt which Kant made to meet it, occupies the greater part of the section. It is aimed at the kind of rationalism prevalent in Hume's time.

Hume points out that any answer must satisfy two requirements.

First, the relations must hold only "betwixt internal actions and external objects". If they held also between "external objects", then inanimate things would be capable of virtue and vice; if they held within the mind, then we "might be guilty of crimes in ourselves, and independent of our situation with regard to the universe". Hume says he cannot think what these relations can be, which require always that one term should be a passion or volition in the mind, the other an external situation, and which can never hold between contents of a single mind, or between external objects alone.

For instance, he says, what is the relation which exists between the will of a parricide and the external situation in which he acts, but is not present in the case of a sapling that outgrows and kills the parent tree from which it sprung? We feel inclined, of course, to say that the difference is that the parricide knows that his victim is his father, but the sapling does not. But Hume would undoubtedly reply that the relation which makes an action virtuous or vicious cannot merely be that the agent knows what the external situation is; for this relation of knowledge is present alike in cases of virtuous, vicious and indifferent actions. It must be some specific kind of knowledge; and if you say that it is knowledge of the rightness or wrongness of the action you argue in a circle, defining right and wrong in terms of the knowledge of right and wrong.

The second requirement, Hume thinks, is even more difficult to fulfil. The relations produced in answer must not only be evidently the same to the understanding of any rational being; it must also be obligatory on the will of any rational being to shape his actions so as to preserve or avoid them, actually do what is "fitting" and avoid what is "unfitting". This necessary connexion between a certain relation of things and the will Hume thinks it will be impossible to discover.

Hume's statement of this requirement (p. 174) is marred by the fact that he assumes that "a is obliged to do x in a situation y" means "The perception of the situation y, or certain features of it, *causes* a to do x". This analysis is doubtful. Nevertheless, the point is otherwise a good one. It is one thing to show that a certain action would have a certain peculiar relation to a certain situation if we did it; it is another to show that *therefore* we *ought* to do it.

The difficulty is the same whether we say that the relation is a mysterious abstract "fittingness", or whether we say that it is that the action would increase human happiness. The question has still to be answered, "Why do what is fitting?" or "Why increase human happiness?" It is the old difficulty, which we have already considered, of the logical step from an "is" or "is not" (or "would be" or "would not be") proposition, to a proposition with an "ought" in it.

The second challenge, addressed to those who think that morality consists in some matter of fact, or empirical feature, discoverable to the understanding, is shortly put on p. 177.

> "Take any action allowed to be vicious; wilful murder, for instance. Examine it in all lights, and see if you can find that matter of fact or real existence, which you call *vice*. . . . In which ever way you take it, you find only certain passions, motives, volitions and thoughts. . . . The vice entirely escapes you, as long as you consider the objects. You can never find it till you turn your reflection into your own breast, and find a sentiment of disapprobation. . . ."

The technique is the same as that which Hume used with regard to the causal relation. The vice and the necessary connexion alike escape you, so long as you consider the objects. You find them when you look into the mind, in the form of a feeling. With these comments, I am content to leave these two challenges to the reader, to take up or not as he pleases.

CHAPTER III

THE ARTIFICIALITY OF JUSTICE
(Treatise Book III, Part II)

1. *Nature, convention and the moral sentiment*

BEFORE giving a detailed account of the moral sentiment, Hume thought it wise to storm the most cherished stronghold of his opponents, the idea of " justice".

His opponents were of two kinds; those who maintained that the principles of justice, being plainly independent of utility and interest (*fiat justitia, ruat caelum*) must be "natural laws"; and those who maintained that they were founded on a "social contract" and therefore, though artificial, not a matter of sentiment.

Both, Hume says, are mistaken. The principles of justice are, indeed, founded on artifices, and are therefore not "natural laws". But they are not founded on any contract, since the keeping of contracts is itself one of the principles of justice. They are founded on customary conventions which command our approbation because of their utility.

This does not commit Hume to the view that all morality is artificial, for virtues other than justice are, he says, useful independently of any conventions, and these may be called "natural virtues".

Before giving his account of justice Hume gives a brief preliminary account of the moral sentiment (Treatise Book III, Part I, Sect. II).

First, he tells us in general, what sort of sentiment it is; approval is a pleasant, and disapproval an unpleasant feeling (p. 178). "The impressions by which good or evil is known, are nothing but *particular* pains or pleasures" (p. 179). But, he observes, "under the term pleasure, we comprehend sensations

which are very different from each other" (p. 180). He gives
as instances the pleasure derived from a good piece of music
and the pleasure derived from a good bottle of wine. Both the
music and the wine are "good" simply because they produce
pleasure; but the different qualities of the pleasures are marked
by the more specific terms of approval we bestow; we call the
wine "of a good flavour", the music "harmonious".

As these two pleasures differ from one another, so does
moral approval differ from either. It is the peculiar pleasure
caused by the character or sentiments of a person, when these
are "considered in general, without reference to our particular
interest".

These different pleasures, he adds, may oppose one another
and may often be confounded one with another; but they do
not wholly destroy one another and remain distinguishable to
careful reflection. Thus, just as personal enmity may make it
difficult, but not impossible, to appreciate the beauty of an
enemy's singing voice, so it makes it difficult, but not impossible, to approve of his moral virtues; or alternatively, the
beauty of a man's singing voice may make it difficult, but never
impossible, to disapprove of his moral vices (p. 180). So much
for the general nature of the moral sentiment.

Secondly, Hume tells us in what way moral judgements are
founded on it. *The moral judgement consists in having the feeling*.
"We do not infer a character to be virtuous, because it pleases;
but in feeling that it pleases after such a particular manner,
we in effect feel that it is virtuous" (p. 179).

This statement is of fundamental importance and gives the
lie to misinterpretations of Hume's doctrine which are very
common. Hume does not say that "the action x is virtuous"
means "the action x causes pleasure by the thought of it to all
or most men". He says that "the action x is virtuous" simply
expresses the sentiment of approval which the speaker feels
when he thinks of x in a certain manner.

Often, of course, we use such expressions to voice feelings
that are not genuine moral sentiments, not generalised and
purged of personal interest; but in such cases we speak
improperly, and do not make genuine moral judgements.

So much for what Hume tells us here of the moral sentiment.
The questions he defers are; what features of the characters

and sentiments of persons cause these feelings of pleasure and pain on a general survey ? and, how do they do so ? The answers to a certain extent emerge as his account of justice proceeds. The answer to the first question is "their utility", the answer to the second question is "by sympathy".

We may now turn to Hume's account of the artificial virtues of justice.

2. *The general argument for the artificiality of justice* (Treatise Book III, Part II, Sect. I)

Hume starts by offering a complicated general proof of the artificiality of justice. This argument may be briefly summarised as follows.

What we approve of and call virtuous or good in an action is always the motive or motives which we presume it to reveal. There must, therefore, be a motive or motives capable of impelling men to perform all actions which we call virtuous, including just actions. This motive cannot be the desire to be virtuous, for this motive presupposes the existence of virtue, *i.e.*, of motives of which we approve. (To say that the motive we approve of is always the desire to do that action of whose motive we approve is to commit an obvious vicious circle.)

But if we take just acts singly we often find them to be such that no normal human motive would impel a man to do them. On the other hand we can find motives for the preservation of the general system of justice, as a form of reciprocal behaviour according to rules. But such a system is plainly something artificial, set up by some convention or agreement among men, or devised by one man or set of men, and forced upon others.

Just actions then are only virtuous because they are in accordance with the system, which is artificial; their virtuousness arises from the contrivances of man, without which they would often not be virtuous, often impossible.

This argument is of special interest in view of a mistake which is alleged by many eminent moral philosophers to be contained in its first two premises. Certain contemporary philosophers, for instance, Sir David Ross in "The Right and the Good", and Mr. E. F. Carritt in "Theory of Morals", draw a distinction between the "rightness" and the "moral goodness" of an action. They say that the latter is dependent on the motive of the action, whereas the former is not. Thus an act can be right, without being morally good, or morally good, without being right. A man for instance may pay his debts, which is right, from fear of going to prison, which is a motive of no moral value; and a man may be carried away by his zeal to fulfil a promise to his dead father, and so ruin his son's prospects, which is wrong, though his motive gives the action moral worth.

These philosophers would admit that for any action to be obligatory or right, there must be some motive capable of impelling the agent to do it; otherwise it would be impossible, and therefore could not be obligatory. But, they would say, there is no vicious circle involved in supposing that the motive may be in some cases, and could be in any case, the desire to do what is right, since right is not defined in terms of motives at all.

Now I agree with these philosophers that when we call an act right, just, obligatory or a duty, we are not saying anything about the agent's motives. Right acts ought to be done however we are feeling, and not only when we happen to be full of pure motives. But I would also agree with Hume that the rightness of the act must be a characteristic which appeals to some normal human motive. Otherwise we should have no reason to wish men to behave rightly, and no reason to expect that they ever would unless it happened to be to their interest to do so in a particular case.

The philosophers in question say that rightness is something unique and undefinable which we "intuite". It is either said to be an intuitable relation of abstract "fittingness" between acts and situations, or defined in terms of an intuitable predicament of "obligedness" in which men find themselves. Hume would rightly ask them how the consciousness of such a relation or predicament could influence the will. Why bother about fittingness or obligation?

Hume could perfectly well do as Mill later did, and do justice to the valid distinction between the right and the morally good, by defining a right act as a useful act, and a morally good act as one done from a desire to be useful, or some other motive which usually leads to useful actions. And it is easy to see, he maintains, what normal human motives prompt us to do and approve of useful actions; *i.e.*, self-interest and sympathy.

Hume's next step is to show that no motive in human nature is capable of impelling us to all the acts which we call just, considered singly and in themselves.

A just act is not always to the agent's own interest; therefore the motive cannot be self-love. Hume, indeed, considers this suggestion to be too absurd to require long consideration (p. 187). The suggestion that the motive is regard to the public interest is more plausible and receives more consideration.

Hume takes the example of repaying a loan. Such an act is not necessarily to the public interest; the debtor might be likely to use the sum more profitably to the public than would the creditor; nor is it always the force of the action as a possible example to others, and therefore a contribution to public security, which provides the incentive of which we approve; for the loan and its repayment may both be secret, and stipulated to be such in the terms of the loan (p. 187). Finally (pp. 187–88), Hume roundly denies that there is in human minds "any such passion as the love of mankind as such, independent of personal qualities, of services, or of relation to ourself".

Lest the reader be too much shocked by this assertion Hume hastens to say that there is, however, such a thing as "sympathy", as a result of which "there is no human, and, indeed, no sensible creature, whose happiness or misery does not in some measure affect us".

This is the first mention of this important force of sympathy on which his whole account of the moral sentiment in the Treatise is to be founded. And the particular point here made in its favour is important. If the principles of morality be founded entirely on human love of human beings as such, all behaviour towards animals, or indeed angels, is as such morally indifferent. The same conclusion would follow if all morality were based on human conventions or contracts, to which animals and angels are not parties, unless the treatment of them were included in the terms of the agreement between men.

But on Hume's view there are natural virtues, independent

of conventions, and founded on sympathy alone; these virtues
cover our treatment of non-human sensible beings. Only the
principles of justice are founded on human conventions and
cover only our treatment of other human beings. Animals
have no rights to property or the observance of contracts; but
it is a virtue to be kind to them.[1]

Finally, Hume says, private benevolence cannot be the
motive; a just act is not always to the interest of the persons
affected by it, still less is it always to the interest of those whom
the agent loves best (p. 188).

Hume concludes that since just acts are not naturally and
in themselves to be desired for any reason, it must be by some
artifice of education and convention that we come to attach so
much importance to them (p. 189).

"In order to avoid giving offence" Hume adds certain
important observations, which anticipate his future arguments
(p. 190). In saying that the sense of justice is not natural, he
only means that it is artificial; he does not deny that it is
natural in the sense of springing from the normal and characteristic workings of the human mind. "Man is an inventive
species", and the inventions which give rise to justice
are the obvious remedies for his natural predicament. It is not,
therefore, improper, Hume says, to call the principles of justice
"Laws of Nature".

3. *The utility of justice and how it was discovered* (Treatise
Book III, Part II, Sect. II; Enquiry, Sect. III)

Hume now proceeds to his positive exposition of the foundations of justice. He begins by asking the following question;
how are "the rules of justice established by the artifice of men"?
(p. 190).

To answer this question Hume has to explain two things:
first, what the motive is that prompts men to establish rules of
justice and observe them, and secondly, how that motive came
to be operative, which it could never have been unless men

---

[1]The distinction between sympathy, which extends to all sentient beings,
and specifically human fellow feeling is not made in the Enquiry. There
the original sentiment on which morality is founded is more often called
"the sentiment of humanity" than "sympathy", and no psychological
account of it in terms of the natural attraction between the idea of a passion
and the passion itself is offered.

had somehow perceived the advantages which justice would confer (p. 192).

The first of these two problems is the more important.

It is a genuinely philosophical problem; the question at issue is not the historical or psychological question, what motives do in fact lead actual men to perform actual just acts ? To this the answer is plainly sometimes one motive, sometimes another; it is rather, to what motive do we mean to appeal when we recommend an action by calling it just ?

The second problem, how men came to perceive the advantages of justice, is, on the other hand, an anthropological question, and Hume is to be congratulated, considering the paucity of anthropological data in his day, on suggesting a plausible answer (experience in family life), and avoiding to a great extent the extravagances of speculative anthropology into which most previous exponents of conventionalist theories of justice and political obligation had fallen. The "State of Nature" and the "Original Contract", or "Social Contract", so dear to Hobbes, Locke and Rousseau, as well as the "Golden Age" of the poets, are, in Hume's view, only convenient fictions.

The original motive to the establishment and observance of justice is, according to Hume, the desire for the material prosperity and personal security which only *society* can confer (p. 191). A man has many needs, food, clothing and housing, all difficult to obtain. By himself he lacks the power and ability to satisfy these needs and protect himself against his natural enemies. Society, by the conjunction of forces, the partition of employments and mutual succour, compensates for these infirmities.

There are, however, certain features of man's nature which are obstacles to the formation and preservation of society (p. 192); these disruptive forces are the "selfishness and confined generosity" of men, which passions are worked upon by the scarcity and easy transferability of those goods the supply of which society is so useful in increasing. Each man loves himself better than anyone else, next best his own family and friends, only third best his "neighbours". He, therefore, tends to grab what he can for himself and his friends, and to induce others to help him in supplying himself with goods, but refuse to help them in return.

M

But he soon discovers that this behaviour defeats its own ends by disrupting society, and that the prosperity of himself and his friends can best be preserved if all members of society observe a set of rules determining the distribution and transference of property and the keeping of promises, which is all that Hume understands to be comprised under the principles of "justice".

This view of the purpose of the principles of justice, though by no means original, is of the greatest importance. If we accept it, we place ourselves at once on the opposite side of the fence to that perennial school of cynical philosophers who hold that nothing can contain the "selfishness and confined generosity of men". Principles of justice, they say, so far from being designed to do so, are merely devices to further the selfishness and confined generosity of the dominant class. "Justice", the Greek Sophist Thrasymachus is reported by Plato to have said, "is the advantage of the stronger"; "Ethical codes", say the Marxists, "reflect the interests of the ruling class".

Hume's second problem is, how do men learn these lessons, and in what way do they put them into effect? They learn these lessons in the family (p. 192); and they put them into effect by convention or agreement (not contract), just as two men row together in a boat by agreement, without any exchange of promises (p. 195).

The family is a miniature society which is natural and not artificial. It arises as a result of the instinctive mutual affection between the parents, and the instinctive concern of the parents for their offspring. Each parent has naturally a concern for the welfare of the other and of the children, and quickly sees how selfishness on the part of either, or of the children, diminishes that welfare. Each parent also sees that though this selfishness is ineradicable it can be rendered to a great extent harmless by the institution and enforcement of rules of property and promise-keeping (p. 198). Their concern for the welfare of each other and the children (as well as themselves) leads them largely to observe these rules and to enforce them on the children by means of their superior strength and power. The keeping of them becomes to a large extent habitual with the children, who, as they grow up, observe the benefits of keeping them and the ill-effects of neglecting them.

Since the family is a natural miniature society, indispensable to the survival of the human species, and since it provides the experience necessary to suggest the advantages of justice and of wider societies, Hume infers that men can never have existed anywhere for any considerable time in "that savage state which precedes society", and probably have always everywhere been to some extent social (p. 198). The lone savage, existing in Hobbes' state of war of all against all, is an abstraction who could scarce have been born or survived to maturity; and society and justice were not the inventions of the *a priori* reasoning of some brilliant pioneer, but the common inferences of all men from experience.

Hume's account of the agreement by which men put these lessons into effect is plausible. When each perceives that to abide by the rules of justice would be for the benefit of all, and makes clear his intention of doing so as long as the others do likewise, justice becomes established. Each successful performance of it encourages others to take the plunge and trust that their fellows will play their part. Hume is clearly right in saying that there is such a process, and that it is not the same as a contract.

Promise-keeping is merely a special case of this process. Each makes clear to each the following intention, "I propose to say *I promise* when I am willing that if I do not perform the action I shall never be trusted again, so long as you use the words with the same meaning". This is the agreement on which the sanctity of promises is founded, according to Hume. It is impossible therefore that the sanctity of promises can be the foundation of all agreements. An agreement is a familiar and intelligible process. A natural sanctity of promises is an unintelligible mystery (pp. 220, 224).[1]

We may define an agreement, on Hume's view, as the

---

[1]It seems to me that, though Hume is right in saying that particular agreements, such as the agreement to adopt certain rules for the distribution of property, are artificial, there may yet be some common instinctive foundation of all agreements. There seem to be instinctive agreements among animals; two horses instinctively stand head to tail, so that the tail of each protects the head of the other from the flies. It is possible that an instinct in men leads them, when faced with a common difficulty or peril, to adopt a general co-operative attitude to one another, by which each expresses a willingness to play his part in some joint action or other, on the supposition that the other will do likewise.

manifestation by two or more persons of a common intention, in which each intends to perform the same or complementary actions so long as the other or others do likewise.

So much for Hume's account of "the manner in which the rules of justice are established by the artifice of men". The motive of *self-interest*, enlightened by the experience of *family life*, leads men to form *agreements* in order to obtain security and prosperity.

4. The "moral beauty" of justice

Hume's next question is, For what reasons we "attribute to the observance and neglect of these rules a moral beauty and deformity". He answers this question briefly on p. 203. The cause is the force of sympathy.

The thought of the benefits and evils that result for men from the observance and neglect of these rules in the vast majority of cases produces by sympathy feelings of pleasure and uneasiness. The essence of the properly moral judgement, as Hume is going to show when he treats of the natural virtues, is that it is the expression of a sympathetically induced pleasure or uneasiness, arising from the contemplation of a character or motive in abstraction from considerations of the contemplator's own particular interests. Our sympathetically induced approval and disapproval of justice and injustice therefore perfectly explain the moral beauty and deformity which we attach to them respectively.

5. Justice and self-interest

(Treatise Book III, Part II, Sects. VI and VII; Enquiry Sect. IX, Part II)

There are two objections to Hume's views which I wish to consider. The first is that Hume implies that the "natural" obligation to justice, founded on self-interest, requires an "inflexible observance of the rules of justice" (pp. 233–35). He implies that it is always, in the long run, really to the interest of the agent to act justly.

The main argument Hume gives to prove this is that only by such inflexible observance can society be preserved, on which the interests of every individual depend.

But it has often been objected to this that what is most to the interest of any given individual is that others should act justly and he alone, or with a chosen gang, act as he pleases. The Greek Sophists maintained that this was what an absolute despot could and did do. He could secure all the advantages of justice by either concealing his own injustice, or forcibly restraining others from imitating it. Plato, in the "Republic", puts the position concretely by endowing his tyrant with a magic ring which makes him invisible at will.

Now Plato sought to prove the fallacy of this contention by showing that justice was the natural and healthy condition of the individual soul as well as of the State. To Hume no such answer is open. There is nothing in the nature of the soul that prompts it to justice, save the intelligence that discovers the conventions necessary for preserving society. And that same intelligence can teach a man how to exploit them to his own advantage.

The passage where Hume most explicitly seeks to prove that honesty always pays the agent is Enquiry Sect. IX, Part II, para. 233. The honest man, he says, besides the pleasures of a good conscience and reputation, "has the frequent satisfaction of seeing knaves, with all their pretended cunning and abilities, betrayed by their own maxims; while they purpose to cheat with moderation and secrecy, a tempting incident occurs, nature is frail, and they give in to the snare; whence they can never extricate themselves, without a total loss of reputation, and forfeiture of all future trust and confidence with mankind".

This is true enough, but hardly meets the objection. Allay conscience with a drug and avoid mistakes, and the difficulty is met.

But Hume has more to say, which I think implies at least one valid answer to our objection:

> "In a view to pleasure, what comparison between the unbought satisfaction of conversation, society, study, even health and the common beauties of nature . . . and the feverish empty amusements of luxury and expense".

Now the pleasures of conversation and society have a more direct connexion with the principles of justice than Hume anywhere explicitly recognises. They depend on open friendly intercourse with one's fellow men; as soon as I have a secret to keep or any need to force men to act against their will, these pleasures are lost. At once I go about with a bridle on my

tongue and my hand on the hilt of my sword, I am back in
Hobbes' "state of nature". And every time I act unjustly this
is the state I am in. For I am acting as other men do not wish
me to behave (we all wish others to be just), and must either
conceal my behaviour or force their acquiescence. This open
fearless intercourse with our fellows is surely more precious
than any of the material gains which dishonesty can win for us.

6. *Justice and the public interest* (Treatise Book III, Part II, Sect. VI)

The second objection I wish to consider is that Hume is
emphatic that the "moral" obligation to justice, founded on
sympathy and public utility, also requires an "inflexible
observance" of the rules of justice (pp. 233–35). But surely
it can be shown that certain acts of injustice are in fact more
beneficial to all concerned than the opposite act.

Take Hume's example: "Here are two persons who dispute
for an estate; of whom one is rich, a fool and a bachelor; the
other poor, a man of sense and has a numerous family". Public
interest plainly requires, on these data, that the estate be
secured to the latter.

Hume answers that the rich fool may nevertheless be the
legal owner; and since property and the rules for its transference are conventions necessary for the existence of
society, it is really to the public interest that the estate be
secured to him.

The objector will reply; "Since the rules of property are
only accepted on account of their utility, surely they would
be more useful if they were only adhered to when it is more
useful to do so, and broken when it is not. Provided the rules
prescribe what is useful in the majority of cases, and are
observed in the majority of cases, society will not be
imperilled".

Hume replies that such loose and flexible rules would
never serve the purpose. Loose rules are indeed useful and
appropriate for a wide field of private and public conduct;
for dress, diet, conversation, entertainment of friends, health,
recreation, etc. But "were men to take the liberty of acting
with regard to the laws of society, as they do in every other
affair (*i.e.*, make exceptions to rules on particular considerations)

. . . this would produce an infinite confusion in human society, and the avidity and partiality of men would quickly bring disorder into the world, if not restained by some general and inflexible principles" (pp. 233-34). In matters of vital common interest we must have universal and inflexible rules, universal because the interests are common, inflexible because the passions excited are so strong and partial that men cannot be trusted to draw exceptions judiciously in the common interest.

Hume does not deny that particular acts of injustice often in fact turn out to the benefit of all concerned. But he does deny that it is possible to form a system or pattern of social conventions which combines these particular benefits with the general benefits of a stable and orderly society. And the latter is far more important. Either you have inflexible rules governing certain matters or you have confusion. If you have inflexible rules, the advantages of occasional unjust acts must be foregone.

The very form of Hume's social conventions implies inflexibility. Each agrees always to behave in a certain way, so long as everyone else always does the same. No one trusts others, or even himself (p. 237), to draw judicious exceptions in the heat of the moment.

If a man has done an unjust act which has in fact conferred great benefits on his country, we may presumably be glad he did it. But our approval is not that generalised approval which is properly moral, and we are not prepared to recommend the act as a model for imitation. A good instance is the act of the Athenian statesman Themistocles who secretly revealed the position and plans of the Greek fleet to the Persian enemy. The Persians as a result attacked the Greek fleet and were disastrously defeated. But can we be sure Themistocles was not partly moved by hope of Persian favour in the event of a Persian conquest, and can we trust others to imitate his example without being misled by that motive to do it when the chances of a victory for their own side are insufficient?

Hume does, however, lay himself open to a misunderstanding; sometimes he speaks of "inflexible rules", sometimes of "inflexible observance of the rules". Now a rule may be in a sense "flexible", even if it is inflexibly observed; it may contain a number of explicit or implicit qualifying clauses, indicating the sort of cases to which it is not meant to apply. And I think it is plain that the principles of justice, both legal and moral, are of this kind.

Suppose I have promised to dine with a friend, and a guest in my house is dangerously ill and I cannot leave him without grave risk. My friend is not on the telephone, and I have no means of asking him to release me from my promise. Does anyone regard himself as party to a social agreement requiring him to keep his promise in such a case? We all know that such exceptions are tacitly provided for in the rule that promises should be kept. If I stay with the sick man I have not broken the rule; I have interpreted it correctly.

Again, suppose a friend is dangerously ill in my house. The wires are down, the roads impassable from snow. Here is a bottle of medicine which will save his life, left in my house by a previous visitor. Is it theft to use the medicine, however valuable? Surely not; the principles of private property tacitly provide for such exceptions. And if the owner of the medicine subsequently sued me at law, it would be open to the courts to mark a technical offence, but dismiss the charge as trifling under the probation of offenders act.[1]

The principles of justice are themselves "flexible", though the observance of them should be "inflexible".

[1] The "flexibility" of legal procedure, under the guiding principle of the public interest, is recognised by Hume in Enquiry, Appendix III, para. 259.

CHAPTER IV

SYMPATHY AND THE NATURAL VIRTUES

(Treatise Book III, Part III, Sect. I; Enquiry, Appendix II)

1. *The psychology of the moral sentiment*

ACCORDING to Hume the sentiments of moral approval and disapproval influence the will and sometimes determine us to action; they must therefore be species of pleasure and pain. For "the chief spring or actuating principle of the human mind is pleasure or pain".

Pleasure and pain give rise to the various "direct passions", *i.e.* "desire and aversion, grief and joy, hope and fear"; we feel grief or joy when the pleasure or pain is actual or certain to become actual, desire and aversion when it is in our power to achieve or to avoid it, hope or fear when it is merely probable, and the mind wavers between belief and disbelief in its existence (Treatise Book II, Part III, Sect. IX, p. 148 *ff.*).

The objects which cause or are expected to cause pleasure or pain may be connected either with ourselves or with others. In the former case they cause also the "indirect" passions of pride or humility (*i.e.* shame), in the latter case those of love or hatred.

Moral approval and disapproval are distinct species of pleasure and pain; the sort that arises from the survey of mental qualities in ourselves or others. All this Hume has said before. It follows, he now points out, that moral approval and disapproval must always be accompanied by pride or humility or love or hatred, as we find them in fact to be.

It is only, Hume repeats (p. 272), "qualities and characters", "durable principles of the mind", which are properly speaking virtuous or vicious, not individual actions. The latter are only styled virtuous or vicious in as far as they are indications of

185

such "durable principles", which alone can actuate the moral sentiment.

The question is, therefore, Hume says, to discover the causes of the pleasure and pain, pride and shame, love and hatred which we feel on the mere survey of the durable qualities and characters of men's minds.

The answer, he says, is sympathy. All men are capable, in varying degrees of the same human feelings; and "when I see the effects of passion in the voice and gesture of any person, my mind immediately . . . forms such a lively idea of the passion as is presently converted into the passion itself. In like manner, when I perceive the causes of any emotion, my mind is conveyed to the effects and is actuated with a like emotion" (p. 272). This is the mechanism of sympathy. The idea of any passion or feeling tends to pass into that very feeling itself, particularly if it is a lively idea, or belief.

Hume does not mean by "sympathy" a mysterious intuitive power of perceiving what is going on in someone else's mind. "No passion of another discovers itself immediately to the mind. We are only sensible of its causes or effects" (p. 273).

This sympathy, Hume claims to have already shown, is the only explanation of our approval and disapproval of justice and injustice; it is also he thinks the principal cause of our love of the beautiful in most cases. It is the tendency to produce happiness, not necessarily our own, which makes us esteem the objects we call beautiful and the artificial systems of justice, modesty and good manners. Our concern for the happiness of others who are not necessarily our friends, can arise only from sympathy (p. 274). "We have no such extensive concern for society, but from sympathy" (p. 275).

Surely then it is probable that sympathy is the cause of those other virtues and vices, whose pleasant and unpleasant consequences, unlike those of justice and injustice, are evident in each individual case, those other virtues and vices, our feelings towards which are generally admitted to be so like those we have for beauty and ugliness.

My first criticism of this argument is that it repeats, for reasons that are not clear, the error we have already noticed;[1]

---

[1] p.p. 173 ff.

i.e. the view that only motives and qualities of character, not acts considered in themselves, are the proper objects of moral judgements. Acts, he says, are only relevant as indications of character.

The reason here given is that qualities of character are sufficiently "durable" to actuate the moral sentiment, acts are not. But why is the moral sentiment only actuated by durable objects? We are not told. Hume could more plausibly have said that only qualities of character, or acts deemed to be evidence of them, are closely enough connected with the person of the agent to actuate the indirect passions of pride and humility, love and hatred. He could then have admitted that acts in themselves could produce approval and disapproval because of their pleasant or unpleasant effects (*i.e.*, their rightness or wrongness), but that only the qualities of character, the virtues and vices, could cause love and hatred, pride and humility. And this is surely the truth.

Indeed, I think a utilitarian must adopt this position, as J. S. Mill later did. For most qualities of character only affect human happiness by the acts they lead to. They cannot, therefore, command our approval unless the acts they lead to command it.

On this view there would be one species of approval, expressed by the word "right", for acts as such, and another species of approval, expressed by the words "virtue", "virtuous", "morally good", for qualities of character and acts regarded as springing from them. The difference would consist in the admixture of pride or love contained in the latter kind of approval but not in the former.

My second criticism is that Hume is unnecessarily egoistic. Let us allow that pleasure and pain form "the chief spring or actuating principle of the human mind". Very well, then it must be pleasure and pain, or the thought of pleasure and pain, which produce moral approval and disapproval, just as they produce desire and aversion, hope and joy, grief and fear. But why should it be only my own pleasure or the thought of it which can arouse a direct passion? Why should not Hume say that pleasure and pain when thought of, not as our own, but as anybody's, arouse directly feelings of approbation and disapprobation? Plainly he thought that this was not true.

It seemed to him self-evident that only what is pleasant or painful to me can arouse in me a passion for or against it. Therefore it seemed to him that the thought of another's pleasure or pain must be converted in my mind by the mechanism of sympathy into an actual pleasure or pain of mine, before it can move my passions and actuate my will.

Now in the Enquiry written ten years later, Hume does take the view that the thought of the pleasures and pains of others directly produces a sentiment in me, which he calls "humanity" or "benevolence", and makes the foundation of moral approval and disapproval.

Moreover, he finds he can say this without wholly abandoning the supposedly self-evident proposition that only what is pleasant or unpleasant to me can, at least on reflection, move my passions; for he finds reason to suppose that the pleasures and pains of others are among the things that are, without any intervention of the sympathy mechanism, pleasant and unpleasant to me. Let us see how he came to form this altered opinion, the germs of which are already present in the Treatise.

If we look at the beginning of the section in the Treatise on "The origin of the natural virtues and vices", we see that Hume does not say that pleasure and pain are the *only* actuating principle of the human mind. He says they are "the chief" actuating principles. What other principles are there, which Hume had in mind?

The others are certain original instincts, such as "desire of punishment to our enemies, and of happiness to our friends; hunger, lust and a few other bodily appetites. These passions, properly speaking, produce good and evil, and proceed not from them, like the other affections" (Treatise Book II, Part III, Sect. IX, p. 149). Similarly, on p. 129, he distinguishes between two kinds of desires, "certain instincts originally implanted in our natures, such as benevolence and resentment, the love of life and kindness to children", on the one hand, and on the other "the general appetite to good and aversion to evil, considered merely as such". "Good" and "evil" in both these passages mean simply pleasure and pain.

By saying that "these passions produce good and evil" he means that their objects, *e.g.*, revenge and food, are pleasant simply because we have an instinctive urge for them; whereas in the case of the other passions, we desire the object because we know or believe it to be pleasant.

These original instinctive desires are what Hume calls "original" as opposed to "secondary" impressions (Treatise Book II, p. 1); they arise from natural and physical causes of which we are not conscious. The secondary or reflective impressions, to which class most of the passions in which Hume is interested are supposed to belong, arise either from the original impressions or their ideas. He does not profess in the Treatise to be much concerned with original impressions; the examination of them belongs to "the sciences of anatomy and natural philosophy" (Treatise Book II, p. 1).

The position in the Treatise is therefore that we have certain original instincts, whose gratification causes pleasure and whose disappointment causes pain. We have also reflective passions, such as hope and fear, joy and grief, pride and shame, which are evoked in various ways by the pleasures and pains produced by the original instincts, or by the thought of those pleasures. What Hume does not seem clearly to have recognised in the Treatise is that since these reflective passions must, on this view, all be dependent on the original instincts and physiological conditions which alone can produce pleasure and pain, the original instincts cannot be ignored, and left to the "anatomists" and "natural philosophers".

By the time he wrote the Enquiry, some ten years later, he had clearly recognised this; consequently, in Appendix II, "Of Self-love", he states a position exactly similar to that of Bishop Butler in his "Fifteen Sermons".[1] Hume now says:

> "There are bodily appetites and wants . . . which necessarily precede all sensual enjoyment, and carry us directly to seek possession of the object. Thus hunger and thirst have eating and drinking for their end; and from the gratification of these primary appetites arises a pleasure, which may become the object of another species of desire, or inclination, which is secondary and interested. In the same manner there are mental passions by which we are impelled immediately to seek particular

---

[1] We know from Hume's letters that he was very anxious to obtain Butler's opinion on the Treatise before publishing it, but was unable to do so. He probably did hear his opinion before he wrote the Enquiry.

objects, such as fame or power or vengeance, without any regard to interest; and when these objects are attained, a pleasing enjoyment ensues, as the consequence of our indulged affections. Nature must, by the internal frame and constitution of the mind, give an original propensity to fame, ere we can reap any pleasure from that acquisition, or pursue it from motives of self-love and desire of happiness. . . . In all these cases there is a passion which points immediately to the object, and constitutes it our good or happiness; as there are secondary passions which afterwards arise and pursue it as part of our happiness, when once it is constituted such by our original affections".

This new point of view, attributing much greater importance to the original instincts, and clearly recognising their disinterested character, led Hume to give a different account of several passions; in the Treatise the love of fame received a complicated account in which sympathy played the principal part (Book II, Part I, Sect. II). In the Enquiry we just have a natural propensity towards fame, and that is the end of the matter. Just as this account is much simpler than the complicated Hobbist account which Hume is arguing against in Appendix II, "Of Self-love", so it is simpler than his own earlier account; and the simpler account, he says, is to be preferred.

On the same principle he adopts a different and simpler account of that concern for the happiness of others which is the foundation of the moral sentiment. In the Treatise "benevolence" is, indeed, regarded as an original instinct; but it is a confined benevolence, a desire for the happiness of our own friends; there is no natural and original love of man for man as such. The concern for the general happiness is due to the mechanism of sympathy, the natural attraction of ideas and impressions. In the Enquiry all this is dropped, and a natural and universal benevolence or "sentiment of humanity" is substituted. The passage quoted above accordingly continues as follows:

"Now where is the difficulty in conceiving that this may likewise be the case with benevolence and friendship, and that, from the original frame of our temper we may feel a desire for another's happiness or good, which, by means of that affection, becomes our own good, and is afterwards pursued, from the combined motives of benevolence and self-enjoyment? . . . What a malignant philosophy it must be, that will not allow to humanity and friendship the same privileges (*i.e.*, being natural or original) which are indisputably granted to the darker passions of enmity and resentment".

Thus, in the Enquiry, the dubious tacit premiss of the argument for sympathy as the basis of the moral sentiment is dropped ; it is not true that our only motive is desire for our own pleasure ; originally we desire whatever our instincts impel us to, which may as well be the happiness of another, as, in the case of vengeance, it is undoubtedly his unhappiness. Secondarily, on reflection, we pursue whatever the gratification of our instincts renders pleasant to us. Sympathy is no longer needed to explain our concern for the happiness of others; an original instinct of humanity is a simpler and, he thinks, truer explanation.

2. *The correction of sympathy in moral judgements*

Hume now proceeds to discuss a threefold objection to his system.

Our sympathy with others, and the same is true of the sentiment of humanity, substituted for it in the Enquiry, varies in proportion to:

(a) The distance in time and place from ourselves of the persons benefited or harmed, and their personal relations to ourselves (p. 277).

(b) The extent to which our own interests are affected by the actions which benefit or harm the persons with whom we sympathise.

(c) The degree of benefit or harm *actually* produced.

But in our moral judgements:

(a) "We give the same approbation to the same moral qualities in China as in England" (p. 277), and we consider the diligence and faithfulness of our own servant no more laudable than the similar qualities of Marcus Brutus (p. 278).

(b) "We overlook our own interests . . ., and blame not

a man for opposing us in any of our pretensions, when his own interest is particularly concerned" (p. 278).

(c) "Virtue in rags is still virtue; and the love which it procures attends a man into a dungeon or desert, where the virtue can no longer be exerted in action, and is lost to the world".

Hume's answer to this objection in all three forms is in essence the same. The moral judgement is sympathetic approval or disapproval corrected by "reason" in a loose and improper sense of the word. This "reason" is "nothing but a general calm determination of the passions, founded on some distant view or reflexion" (p. 279).

The *motive* to adopt this general distant viewpoint and the calm and steady passions it arouses, is the dislike we have for the constant fluctuations and contradictions which arise in our sentiments, and the confusions which arise in society and conversation, when we feel and speak in a manner determined solely by the particular, changeable and accidental circumstances of the case in question (pp. 277–79).

It would be most inconvenient if, even where there were no doubt about the facts, I called a given act right and you called it wrong one moment, and a little later I called it wrong and you called it right, owing to the differences and changes of our personal relations to the agent and the persons affected. It would be most inconvenient if of two essentially similar acts one was called virtuous and the other vicious because of differences in accidental circumstances possibly unknown to the agent.

The *method* of achieving this general and distant viewpoint is by means of the imagination. I imagine myself as near in time and place to Marcus Brutus as I am to my servant, and as distant from my servant as I am from Marcus Brutus; I imagine myself as disinterested when in fact I am interested; I imagine the benefits usually conferred by a certain mental quality, ignoring the peculiar impediments attaching to the particular case.

"The imagination has a set of passions belonging to it" Hume says (p. 280). These exercises of the imagination produce a passion uninfluenced by the accidental and peculiar circumstances of the case. It is not really a passion with an imaginary object, though Hume's language rather suggests this (p. 280). The action or character is still real; but it is imagined with its accidental and variable qualities and relations removed or changed. The generous man in the dungeon still really has a generous mind; he is only imagined to be free, instead of in a dungeon, in order that I may feel the passion appropriate to generosity in general, not generosity in chains.

The *emotional response* to the generalised view of the object is sympathy. "Being thus loosened from our first station (the particular view), we cannot afterwards fix ourselves so commodiously by any means as by a sympathy with those who have any commerce with the person we consider".

Now whatever we may think of Hume's account of sympathy or of humanity, whatever we may think of his equation of the good with the pleasant, there can be no doubt·that there must be some passion which moves us to approve of certain ends and the actions and characters which usually tend to achieve them, and there can be no doubt that this passion is in fact generalised and rendered impersonal and impartial very much in the way Hume describes. I regard Hume's account of "that reason which is able to oppose our passion" (p. 279) by generalising it in the interests of stability, coherence and the intelligibility of language, as one of the most valuable suggestions to be found in his philosophy. My only objection is to his saying that this use of the term "reason" is loose and improper. On the contrary, it seems to me that this is just the sort of mental process which we usually and properly call "being reasonable".

It has been argued against Hume that there may be several different principles or motives underlying the generalised approvals and disapprovals of men, and that some men may be exclusively moved by one and some by another. Thus Professor C. L. Stevenson in "Language and Ethics" (pp. 273 ff.) says that Hume makes the dubious assumption that if all differences in opinion on questions of fact were removed, everyone would agree in their attitudes of approval and disapproval; and that this is because Hume confines himself to the consideration of "benevolent attitudes", which is, in effect, not to offer an impartial analysis of moral judgements as they are actually made, but to preach an Ethics of Benevolence.

N

I think such a criticism ignores much of what is most important in Hume's system. It is, indeed, the suggestion of certain very condensed passages in the Enquiry (the only work of Hume's to which Professor Stevenson refers) that if all differences on questions of fact were removed, men's attitudes, in as far as they were not influenced by self-love or passions due to particular features of particular cases, would be determined solely by benevolence. But it is quite clear from the passages in the Treatise which we have been considering, and also from Enquiry, para. 221, that this suggestion is not a bare assumption. Hume offers us a more precise analysis than Professor Stevenson ever does of the purpose for which we use ethical terms. Their tendency, he says, is towards universal agreement in attitude (approval or disapproval) about human actions and qualities of character. They are used to make recommendations for universal adoption. Now a recommendation presupposes in the person or persons to whom it is addressed some motive or motives to which appeal is made. A universal recommendation therefore presupposes a universal motive or motives, which will make all men accept that recommendation. Benevolence (or sympathy) would make all men accept the same recommendations; benevolence is present, however weak, in all normal men. No other human motive that Hume can think of would produce this agreement. Therefore, Hume argues, all genuine moral judgements make appeal to benevolence, and make recommendations on grounds of general utility.[1]

The possibility of divergent fundamental attitudes is considered by implication in the Treatise (Book III, Part III, Sect. I, p. 279).

What Hume there says is, not that benevolence or sympathy is the *only* principle by which we can determine our attitudes after being loosened from our first partial and biased "station", but that "we cannot afterwards fix ourselves *so commodiously* by any means as by a sympathy with those who have any commerce with the person we consider". Hume is suggesting that other

---

[1] Men do, of course, from various motives praise useless and blame harmless actions. But their procedure is futile. The retort "Why? What good (or harm) does it do anyone?" finds them without an answer. Just as, when men blame or punish unavoidable actions, the retort "But he could not have avoided it" is, as Professor Stevenson recognises, conclusive.

motives by which men might determine their generalised approvals and disapprovals would have disadvantages, which sympathy (or benevolence) alone lacks.

Let us consider what these disadvantages could be.

Suppose somebody prefers to fix his moral judgements by saying that all actions and characters should be judged by their tendency to retard or accelerate the inevitable emergence of a world-wide classless society, or the evolution of the superman, or the spread of Christianity. We know men do, in fact, do this; and we know what confusion, disagreement and inconvenience their resultant conflicting attitudes produce.

Now, according to Hume, it is precisely the dislike of confusion, contradictions, etc., that led men to seek some general and impartial standpoint. Therefore, that same dislike of confusion which required the abandonment of conflicting and unstable, personal and interested standpoints, will require the correction of the conflicting generalised standpoints by some universally acceptable one. And the only standpoint which will do the job, he says, is sympathy (benevolence).

Now it may be objected that it is just as true that all men would agree in their moral judgements (differences on questions of fact being resolved) if they were all good Marxists or all good Christians or all good Nietzscheans, as it is that they would all agree if they were all good Utilitarians; where then is the superiority of the benevolence principle?

To this I think there are two answers.

First, that the other principles cited, and probably most others that could be cited, rest on factual beliefs; that the classless society is inevitable, that the doctrine of Evolution is true, that Jesus Christ was the son of God, and so on. They are, therefore, not genuine principles for fixing attitudes *after* the elimination of factual disagreements.

Second, it is not enough that a principle would in theory produce agreement if adopted by all; it is also necessary that there should be some hope of getting it adopted by others, and sticking to it myself. And there is no such hope unless there is some motive present in all normal men at most times capable of impelling them to adopt it.

Obviously there is no motive capable of impelling members of the bourgeoisie to adopt the Marxist principle; except possibly benevolence, if they can be persuaded that the classless society would be the happiest. Nor is there really any motive capable of impelling the weak to adopt a principle requiring their elimination in order that the strong may more quickly generate supermen; except possibly benevolence, if they can be persuaded that the race of supermen would be the happiest form of humanity.

But the benevolence principle itself makes no factual assumptions, and appeals not only to the motive of benevolence itself, but also to self-love; it is difficult to see what other principle could make a greater appeal to self-love. *Ex hypothesi* not all my wishes can be gratified without a fight, since some of them conflict with the wishes of others; *ex hypothesi* I dislike fights (otherwise I would not bother to make moral judgements); what other principle has more to promise than the principle that the happiness of all concerned should be maximised, the wishes of all gratified as far as possible? It is a choice in the end between this principle and perpetual conflict, within my own mind, and between myself and others. If there is another alternative, to use Hume's words, "I desire that it may be produced".

This is philosophising, not preaching. Here is first an analysis of the facts; when we make moral judgements we express feelings for and against, feelings so generalised and impartialised that they can serve as common bases for practical agreement. And secondly, here is a challenge; how else, but by the benevolence principle, can you get feelings suitable to be a basis of practical agreement? That is the Humean way of philosophising; a combination of the experimental method with the method of challenge.

Before leaving Hume's theory of morals, there is an amendment I would like to propose to it; an amendment which, if carried, would I think not be in the least damaging to his general position.

It will be noticed that in the last few pages I have, following Professor Stevenson's usage, tended to use the term "attitude", where Hume would have said "sentiment of approval or disapproval". Hume seems to have thought that the moral sentiment was a perfectly specific introspectible feeling of pleasure or pain. It is, I think, rightly objected by many modern philosophers that it is not possible to find and identify this specific feeling.

If moral approval and disapproval were specific feelings, then the degree of moral approval or disapproval should vary with the intensity of this feeling. But in fact it seems to be to a large extent independent of degree of intensity of any feeling. Therefore, Professor Stevenson and others prefer to speak of "attitudes" rather than "sentiments", and to define attitudes as dispositions to speak, feel and act in certain ways.

My proposed amendment is, therefore, to substitute the term "attitude", defined as above, for "sentiment" or "feeling" throughout. Do this, and Hume's main position remains unshaken. Moral decisions consist not in the discovery of any empirical or demonstrable facts, but in our attitudes towards the facts. When all questions of fact have been settled, the moral question remains, what is our attitude, or, perhaps better, by what stable, universal and general attitude can our more particular attitudes be corrected, harmonised and rendered consistent with one another.

I have, in effect (see my p.   ), proposed a similar amendment to Hume's theory of belief. Belief is not a specific introspectible way of imagining or feeling attached to images. It is a disposition to feel, imagine, speak and act in the way that would satisfy my needs if the propositions I believe were true.

Hume was, I think, right in thinking that belief and moral approval were the same sort of thing, right in thinking that each tended to be corrected and harmonised by general rules in the same sort of way. Just as the influence on the mind of general utility, appealing to benevolence and enlightened self-love, corrects and harmonises our moral approvals and disapprovals, so does the influence on the mind of the general run of experience as a whole correct and harmonise our factual beliefs.[1] But he was not quite right in his account of what sort of thing belief and moral approval are. They are not exactly "sentiments"; they are dispositions; dispositions actualised partly but not exclusively in feelings.

[1] If this is true, the principles of Utilitarian Ethics, if they could be worked out as, for instance, Bentham tried to work them out, would be related to ethical judgements in the same way as the principles of Inductive Logic are related to empirical judgements of fact.

APPENDIX

FREEDOM OF THE WILL

(Treatise Book II, Part III, Sects. I & II; Enquiry concerning
Human Understanding, Sect. VIII)

HUME sides definitely with the determinists in this ancient
controversy, but in a manner peculiarly his own. These
sections are notable for the rigorous consistency with which
he applies his doctrine of causation to the question. The
conclusion to which this method leads him is that the controversy is unreal and rests on confusions which are mainly
terminological.

All men have ever been agreed, he says, that human actions
are necessary and determined in one sense, which is the proper
sense, and have only been inclined to deny that they are
determined in another sense, to which he says no clear meaning
has ever been assigned.

Similarly, all men have ever been agreed that human actions
are free in one sense, but that sense has been confused with
another sense of the word "freedom", in which it is absurd to
say they are free.

The issue has been complicated, he says, by theological
considerations. In the Treatise we read that theology has been
"very unnecessarily interested in this question", i.e., has
meddled in philosophy. In the Enquiry he affects greater
politeness to theologians; he censures philosophy for her
"temerity" in prying into the "sublime mysteries" of religion.
His tone is undoubtedly ironical, if not sarcastic.

All men have ever agreed, Hume says, in thinking human
actions to be necessary and to have causes. That is, according
to his view of cause and necessity, they have (a) always found
constant conjunctions between men's actions and their motives,
and between their motives and their situations, tempers, sex,

upbringing, nationality, etc.; and (b) they have always made inferences concerning human actions in accordance with their experience of this regularity.

Now this is all they have in fact been able to do with regard to inanimate objects; our reasonings concerning human actions and physical processes are on exactly the same footing. In each case, where irregularities are found, the same presumption is made with the same degree of justification, that if all the facts were known the apparent irregularity would be found to be due to contrary causes. The mistake men have made is to suppose that in physical events they can discover some objective necessity, something more than mere regularity in the object and determination of their own thought about it; then, turning to human actions and introspecting their own behaviour, they have announced that they cannot find this objective necessity there, and that human actions are therefore "undetermined".

Men have ever agreed, Hume says, that human actions, or some of them, are free, *i.e.*, have the liberty of spontaneity. What we do depends on what we choose to do, on our thoughts and wishes. The opposite of this freedom is compulsion, as ordinarily understood. But they have confused freedom of spontaneity with freedom of indifference, *i.e.*, the absence of a cause, or chance; and consequently have tended to assert that human actions are not caused, which is absurd.

Libertarians, according to Hume, have supported their muddle-headed contention by three arguments.

(I) An appeal to a delusion of introspection (Treatise, p. 121, Enquiry, para. 72, footnote). Though we commonly regard human actions, when viewed from the outside, as due to psychological causes, and so determined, when we reflect on a present or very recent action of our own, it seems to us, for two reasons, that we could equally well have done the opposite. First, we find that we can equally easily imagine ourselves doing the opposite, for instance raising an arm instead of lowering it; this is presumably because we have as often raised our arm as lowered it in the past. Secondly, we find that on repeating the experiment, we can raise the arm instead of lowering it, though the circumstances are, we think, identical. But, Hume points out, the circumstances are not identical. For there is now present a motive which was absent before, *i.e.*, the desire to show our liberty by raising our arm. And this is the cause of our raising it.

This passage in Hume is a very penetrating piece of analysis, and his discovery a special case of a more general truth which has since been widely recognised as having an important bearing on the question of the freedom of the will.

This general truth is that a human action is liable to be affected by any thought that the agent may have about it, including his thought that he is or is not certain or likely to do it. A consequence of it is that, though human actions have their causes as much as physical events, they are not in principle predictable in the same way. For the thought that I am bound to do a certain action may touch off motives which will prevent me doing it; and the thought that another man is bound to do something may lead me to communicate to him thoughts about that action which will prevent him doing it. I may, for instance, tell him that his dead father would have been very shocked if he could see him do it.

Human actions are thus unpredictable in principle in a way that physical events are not, and dependent on human thoughts in a way that physical events are not. But these facts do nothing to show that our actions and our thoughts do not take place according to causal laws.

(II) A delusive appeal to moral considerations (Treatise, p. 122 ff., Enquiry, paras. 75–77). The argument is that if human actions are all causally determined, they cannot have any merit or demerit, or deserve reward and punishment, praise and blame.

Hume argues that the liberty of spontaneity is, indeed, necessary for moral responsibility, but the liberty of indifference would entirely destroy it. Unless human actions were caused by the motives, characters, and temperaments of the agents, if they were mere disconnected flukes, however deplorable and unfortunate they might be, they would not be proper objects of the passions of anger and hatred on which vengeance is founded. And unless they were affected by the thoughts and wishes and fears of the agents, rewards and punishments would be quite ineffective in controlling them.

This argument, says Hume, applies equally to human and

divine rewards, punishments, and vengeance. Moral responsibility therefore does not presuppose the freedom of indifference. It presupposes merely that a man's actions should be partly determined by his thoughts and feelings about them and their consequences. When we do not think this is so, as in the case of a kleptomaniac, we do not regard the man as responsible for his actions, and consider blame and punishment inappropriate, simply because they are useless (Treatise Book III, Part III, Sect. IV, p. 302).

(III) Theological considerations (Enquiry, paras. 78–81). These difficulties Hume does not claim entirely to "obviate or remove" (para. 78); the failure does not worry him very much, since theologians have been quite unable to reconcile "the indifference and contingency of human actions with prescience" (and, he should have added, with omnipotence) (para. 81), and, consequently, there are just as strong theological arguments against libertarianism. Philosophy should leave divine mysteries alone and return to "the examination of common life; where she will find difficulties enough" (para. 81).

Hume does, however, do something to weaken the theological argument against determinism. The argument is really a dilemma; "If human actions can be traced up, by a necessary chain, to the Deity", then *either* God is perfect, and nothing that is originated by him can be evil, in which case no human actions are evil, and there is no such thing as guilt or sin, *or* human actions are criminal, and God as their ultimate author must be held guilty of them (para. 78). Hume suggests an answer to the first horn of the dilemma. I think he might have suggested answers to both, had he not been unwilling to embroil himself in theological controversy.

The answer he suggests to the first horn of the dilemma is as follows: "There are philosophers who conclude", he says (but does not say he believes them) "that the whole, considered as one system, is, in every period of its existence ordered with perfect benevolence. . . . Every physical ill makes an essential part of this benevolent system, and could not possibly be removed, even by the Deity himself, . . . without giving entrance to greater ill". The same may be presumed to be true of moral ill (para. 79).

Now, if this is so, Hume says, God is plainly exculpated;

but it does not follow that the evils which are necessary parts of the good whole are therefore not evil. The Stoics, he says, had tried to maintain that physical evils, such as pain, were not really evils, on just these grounds; and nobody in practice was much consoled by them. On the contrary, from the operation of the psychological principles, which Hume has described, we shall still continue to disapprove of vice because of its disagreeable effects, whatever we may think of its ultimate origin. We shall still disapprove of the vicious characters necessarily included in the world. And if we really disapprove of them they really are vicious.

As regards the second horn of the dilemma, it might seem that Hume could have said that we shall still wholeheartedly approve of God for making the best of all possible worlds, even if we disapprove of the vicious characters necessarily included in it; and if we really do wholeheartedly approve of God, he really is perfectly good. Hume, however, does not commit himself to this heterodox opinion.

What he actually says elsewhere[1] is that the moral sentiments have their origin in human nature and human society. Virtues and vices are human qualities pleasing and unpleasing to human spectators. God is not a human being; there is, therefore, no more sense in calling him unjust or unkind than there is in calling an alligator unjust or unkind. Experience affords no evidence that the Creator's sentiments are at all similar to ours. It suggests rather that they are very different, since he has made a world so very different from any that we should have wished to make.

---

[1] "Dialogues concerning Natural Religion", Parts XI and XII., J. Hill Burton, "Life and Correspondence of David Hume", Vol. I, p. 119.

INDEX